Becoming a Successful Tax Agent

Terence S. McNamara

Contributions by:

Ambe Claudius
Tamara Zagami
Mary Tawil
TAP Media

Inspiring Publishers
P.O. Box 159, Calwell, ACT Australia 2905
Email: publishaspg@gmail.com
http://www.inspiringpublishers.com

A catalogue record for this
book is available from the
National Library of Australia

NATIONAL
LIBRARY
OF AUSTRALIA

National Library of Australia The Prepublication Data Service

Author: Terence S. McNamara
Title: Becoming a Successful Tax Agent
Genre: Non-Fiction

Paperback ISBN: 978-1-923449-53-4
ePub2 ISBN: 978-1-923449-54-1

DEDICATION

Thank you to my editors and contributors Ambe Claudius, Tamara Zagami, Patricia Turco, all successful Tax Agents, and to Mary Tawil, the Operations Manager at Tax Agent Pathway. Also, a thank you to our media company TAP Media.

BECOMING A TAX AGENT

And create a successful tax practice.

Contents

PREFACE

This is not a textbook about tax law or accounting theory, although those matters do form part of the text. This volume is about what you do to obtain your Tax Agent license and want to enter the tax preparation and accounting profession by starting your own practice. We will review part of the tax law and accounting theory as it pertains to being a professional in public practice, and how it affects you in the pursuit of running a successful practice. This book is primarily about the myriad of issues and exposures that likely have not been covered in your academic studies. Here we cover all the things that you will need to know about running a successful practice and becoming a productive and sort-after tax practitioner.

CHAPTER ONE

Preparation

Being a Tax Agent brings with it responsibilities and obligations, and you need to be prepared to commit to staying up to date with the legislation and acquiring the ancillary knowledge needed to properly service your clients when you are running a practice. We will cover off on all of those requirements in this text but first and foremost, you need to remember that when in public practice you are managing a business. You are no good to your clients, or the ATO, if you bankrupt yourself. The first key to being successful in business is preparation and planning. Here are some key issues related to planning for a healthy accounting business that you should undertake at the outset.

Groucho Marx said, 'budgeting is a way of going broke methodically'. In part that is true, if you rely too much on speculation in your budgets as opposed to facts. At the beginning you personally won't have too many actuals on which to base your planning but that doesn't mean that the information is not available. You are not the first person to go into practice. Do your research. As you move forward pay close attention to the actual numbers that emerge in your profit and loss, they are critical to your forward planning.

Don't ever base your expenditure on what you think is going to happen. Spending money today based on figures you projected in your spreadsheet is fraught with danger. Spreadsheets are terribly addictive and can be a poisonous way of managing your business. By all means project and plan but understand that the future part of those sheets is fiction. Value actuals and industry benchmarks above what you would like the future numbers to look like. You want those future numbers to be true, you believe they will be true but they are sand, you can't construct your future on sand. Start with what you believe to be true, backed up by rigorous industry research. Be conservative when projecting a financial plan and have an eye on unforeseen setbacks or changes in economic conditions.

Below that, develop a step-by-step set of actions to achieve that plan. Each step that you achieve—update your plan, which is part of the reason that you need to break your plan down into baby steps. Don't let the ultimate objective intoxicate your next step. Stay clear headed. Let your next result inform each subsequent step.

One of your first key decisions is your pricing and deciding what is your target market. You can't project sales unless you first decide to whom you are selling your services and what you are going to charge for those services. Also look closely on the mix of services you are going to provide. Building a practice on personal tax returns does not make for a successful and profitable practice long-term. Let the personal returns come your way organically, through friends, contacts, recommendations and, more importantly, the work you do for small businesses. The government is doing its best to eliminate personal tax returns or, at the very least, to make the process of lodging a personal return so simple as to remove the need for a Tax Agent.

Also, Individual Tax Returns (ITRs) are price sensitive, which brings us to the next key lesson here: do not under any circumstances be cheap. Cheap in this industry is equated to being nasty. Cheap accountants are seen as backyarders who don't keep up with best practices and don't make enough money to fully service their clients. Besides, acquiring a client on price alone will not build your business for two reasons: firstly, they will shop you next year for sure, there will always be some other idiot who is cheaper than you, so they will leave you and all that set-up work you did for them, for no financial gain, will be out the window. Secondly, cheap clients are almost always the most demanding even though they are not paying you much, their very nature is to seek to get as much as they can out of you in order to get the most service for their money. There is no profit to be made properly servicing cheap clients.

Not being cheap is doubly important when operating in your key market: small business. The small businessperson primarily wants to get it right and is prepared to pay the right amount of money to get it right. If your prospective client is focused on cheap services or wants to cheat the tax law to save money, send them away. They will get themselves and you into trouble, and you definitely don't want to be part of that process. Most small businesspeople want to get it right and they are smart enough to understand that it is false economy to use a cheap accountant. They want the right tax result, so they want one that uses best practice to get the lowest legal tax result for the client. You don't want your client facing an audit, so make sure you diligently seek out the correct numbers. Time to get it right costs money, so make sure you have enough margin in your pricing to spend on each client. An audit that yields errors will reflect badly on you with the ATO as well as possibly lose you the client.

I once had an association with a very large food production company who had one major competitor. Both companies were struggling to make decent profits because they were constantly at each other's throat, undercutting the other's prices. The company I was associated with had a change of CEO who immediately put their prices up twenty percent and the company's sales volume went up significantly, not down. He did it again getting the same result with another twenty percent price hike. It was an important lesson for me early in my career. The customer buying what were almost identical products offered by the two companies believed that the higher price meant better quality ingredients. The product formula in my client's product never changed, just the price.

Go cheap, go broke.

Do a cashflow and watch it like a hawk. Don't live on the edge of your cashflow. One hiccup and you're flat on your face. Banks don't help businesses that are flat on their face regardless of previous performance, they only help businesses that don't need their help.

Other than self-interest and the pursuit of profitability, you need to be part of the industry that is providing value and quality advice to their clients. Don't be part of the problem, be part of the solution. You can't spend the time and money to stay up to date, spend sufficient time on your returns to be thorough and be able to afford quality staff, if you don't have the profit margins to support those objectives. You have a responsibility to your clients, to the ATO and to your profession to contribute to the wellbeing of your clients and, in so doing, ensure their accurate compliance with the tax law. If you can't do the right thing, choose another business.

The average taxpayer, particularly one operating a small business, expects you to be all knowing. That means two things: firstly, stay on top of tax law developments by investing in continued study, and secondly, have a network of experts that can help you with difficult cases. The ATO expects you to know what you are doing, so does your client. If you don't, they both will eventually come and get you. You need to be committed to providing a complete and well-informed service. Yes, there are Tax Agents out there that don't fit the criteria but their days are numbered. Build a practice and build your asset on sound principles.

Importantly, don't just be a form filler. You can't just put a number in a box presented to you by your tax software. You must know whether that number is right, where it comes from, whether it is legitimate, that it has been reconciled and fully supported and whether it provides the best legal tax result for your client. As a public practitioner the ATO does not expect you to audit your client's books but they do expect you to be 'diligent', and, these days, being diligent covers a lot of ground. The ATO will not advise your client on legal ways to minimise the client's tax, that's your job.

When factoring in the cost of software into your budget, understand the difference between paying for ledger software and paying for tax software. Ledger software is the software used by your clients to do their bookkeeping. It is important that the client pays for that subscription, not you, because you want your client to own that data. If you own the ledger data and you leave or get fired, explain to your client at the outset that they need to be able to keep their data, so they need to pay for the ledger software subscription. You, however, must pay for the software that assists you to prepare and lodge the returns. Make sure your tax software accepts exports from the major ledger programs.

You may also want to consider software that assists you to manage your practice, such as client profitability management, debtors and time sheets but frankly that should not be a priority when you are starting out, but consider it when you are fully established.

Use ledger software for your own bookkeeping, that will cover off on much of the management information that you require to run your practice if you set up your chart of accounts in sufficient detail.

Above all of that, understand the numbers that you are putting into whatever software you are using.

CHAPTER TWO

What You Need to Obtain Your Tax and BAS Agent's License

To become a Tax Agent in Australia you must be at least eighteen years of age, or so it says in the Act but I can't see how at eighteen you could have obtained the requisite academic and experience qualifications. You must also be a fit and proper person, which means you can't be bankrupt or a felon, and you need to satisfy the qualifications and experience requirements as set out in the Tax Agent Services Regulations 2022, referred to herein as TSAR or the Act (see later Chapter for more details).

Those requirements to become a Tax Agent then fall into two broad categories: academic qualifications and relevant experience under the supervision of a Tax Agent. Academically the Tax Practitioners Board, the TPB, wants you to have what they refer to as *primary qualifications* which is a diploma or degree. But that requirement can be distilled down to board approved courses in basic accounting (one unit), Australian tax law (two units) and Australian commercial law (three board approved core units). Plus, they will require you to have completed a unit in ethics as codified in TSAR which has to have been completed within the five years immediately prior to your application to be licensed because those regulations are constantly updated.

Whilst it is not specifically itemised in TSAR, you should ensure that your accounting courses fully cover off on bookkeeping, we'll deal with this more completely in a later chapter. If you can't prepare and reconcile a ledger then you are never going to understand the numbers presented to you in your client's business accounts. If you don't understand and have not verified the numbers coming out of your client's business accounting systems, then you are going to get the tax return wrong. The ATO requires that you be diligent in verifying the numbers you are using. I would recommend that you include a Certificate IV in bookkeeping in your academic qualifications.

Before choosing which course to undertake make sure that it contains all board approved units and that it is provided by an accredited college. If you already have some tertiary qualifications, then the best way to determine if your current qualifications are adequate is to call one of the accredited educational institutions, speak to their Tax Agent training area, tell them what you already have and they will tell you any additional units that you will require. For time management purposes you are best advised to only do the specified units that you are missing rather than seek a further diploma or degree on top of what you already have obtained.

Regarding experience, you will need around fourteen hundred to eighteen hundred hours of tax preparation work conducted under the supervision of a registered Tax Agent. It may be more or less than that depending on your qualifications and what commercial or accounting work you have done outside of preparing tax returns. Much of the TPB literature talks about chronological time spent preparing returns under supervision but they typically measure your experience by the hours you have spent preparing returns because you may be working full-time or part-time. The experience needs to include preparation of a variety of returns, that is personal, company, trust, partnership and self-managed super fund returns. There is no specification available as to how many of each return types you will need to have completed other than to say that you need a spread of experience obtained within the required hours of work.

The acquisition of that experience does not need to be full time but it needs to be obtained in the five years leading up to your application to be licensed. When working under the supervision of a Tax Agent, it is advisable that you get their written commitment to certify your experience hours before you start working with them. Causal arrangements, part-time or full-time, working under supervision can end badly when it comes time for the Tax Agent to certify your experience hours. Remember, fundamentally they won't want you to compete with them especially if you have obtained your experience working with their clients.

Tax Agent Pathway (www.taxagentpathway.com.au), TAP, is the largest independent supervisor of tax return preparation services in Australia either part-time or full-time. They specialise in the provision of that service and they don't offer tax services to the general public, therefore, they have no conflict with the services you provide to your clients. You will need to find your own clients but you'll need to do that in any case as you build your practice. With TAP you will be operating under highly qualified professionals within a secure environment of a specified set of obligations between the supervision provider and you, the tax preparer seeking experience.

It seems that it is not a requirement of the TPB for you to be a member of an accredited professional organisation. I say *seems to be* because the answer to that question varies depending on with whom you are speaking. If you are talking to one of the professional associations, they will tell you that it is a requirement, if you talk to the TPB they will not confirm or deny that it is a requirement. It is, however, well regarded by the TPB that you are a member and if you are a member, it may impact on the number of hours you are required to work when obtaining your relevant experience. Either way you are required by the TPB to do ongoing professional development hours. You must keep up to date with changes in the tax law. The best providers of that professional development education tend to be the TPB accredited professional bodies. Most bodies also have some kind of technical support and technical literature including regular newsletters. TAP also provides that support.

It will, in the end, be of value to you to be a member of one of those bodies. That is also true when it comes to obtaining your Professional Indemnity (PI) insurance. The TPB will require you to have PI insurance before they grant you your license, the amount of cover you will require will depend on the size of your practice but they will start you out at $250,000 in cover if you are starting from scratch. Most of the accredited professional associations offer discounts on PI insurance to their members which increases the value to you of being a member. Refer to the ATO website for a list of those accredited entities but the largest three are the IPA, CPA and CA.

Several people seeking a Tax or BAS Agent's license tend to get confused between what the TPB requires and what their professional accounting association requires from them to be a *public practitioner*. It is important that you understand the distinction. The TPB does not require you to have done a *Public Practice Certification* course from any of the professional associations, that is only required by some of the professional associations in order for you to practice under their credentials. If you wish to put yourself forward in the marketplace as being a CPA, or CA or IPA practice you will need to talk to the relevant body to determine what they require from you that will enable you to use those designations in your signage, emails, website and promotions. You can still be a member of any society without promoting your practice under their credentials but some have restrictions and requirements if you are going to trade under their credentials. Typically, those that do have restrictions will require you to obtain some kind of public practice certificate.

It is important for you to understand what the protected designations in Australia are, that is, the names that you can legally call yourself. The term 'Tax Agent' and 'BAS Agent' are protected names by law, you can't refer to yourself as either unless you are licensed. The terms *accountant, tax accountant,* or *bookkeeper* are not protected. The designations CPA, CA and IPA, as previously mentioned, are protected by copywrites registered by those respective societies, not by ATO tax law but by general business law.

CHAPTER THREE

Marketing and Promotions

Starting a business is a daunting task for most people but there are some tried and true techniques which can be used to ensure you maximise your opportunities.

First and foremost, as a public practitioner you need to develop a basic business marketing plan outlining your objectives and some estimates of costs you are going to incur to achieve those objectives. That means how to get your business to a point where it is commercial, generating a wage for yourself as well as a profit. Being financially literate, you can work through the costs for the first year of business and the level of activity that you must achieve in order to breakeven.

Always remember that above all else you are running a business, that you are a small business owner, and most small business owners look at the most conservative scenario of total costs to operate for a year, particularly your first year. You will then know what margin you need in your pricing and what level of marketing activity you need to achieve the projected sales. Looking at other practitioners operating in your market area will help enable you to develop a pricing scenario that will work for your business but as previously mentioned, do not be the cheapest. So, it is important, at least in the beginning, to get involved with local discussion groups with your fellow practitioners. Ask them what they are spending on marketing and how they are executing their promotional plans. Look at their websites and review the pitch they are making to their prospective clients. In doing that, however, always shape those ideas through the lens of what is right for you in your current circumstances, all the time understanding and carefully deploying what capital you have available.

Don't overspend on non-essential promotion or website embellishments. Look to put a clear message out there and provide a definitive offer to the clients you are seeking.

Sadly, many businesses do not consider the question of marketing and promotional costs and the planned execution of your objectives adequately enough but it is vital if you are to grow and prosper. In this chapter we will look at some of the variables you might consider as you embark on your new journey as a practitioner.

Fundamentally, once you have selected a name for your business, you need to register the URL for that name, after you have registered the name with ASIC or successfully created a company using that name. Then engage with a local graphics designer to assist you in the development of a logo, graphics package, including business cards, stationery, invoices and email signatures. You should apply your logo consistently across all media including emails and your website. This does not have to be expensive, particularly if you give the designer clear written guidance on the sort of look you are trying to achieve. A good brief will generally result in a good design at a lower cost.

In selecting your business name consider the way that the Google search engine works. For a start, it will always select Australian businesses first if the searcher is looking from Australia, which yours will mostly be doing, so do not use '.com' by itself, instead use '.com.au' or just '.au.' when registering the URL for your business name, perhaps buy both. Google will also look at relevance, that is, how close is your business name to what the Google user is asking for in their search. So, including *taxation* or *accounting* in the name is always advisable.

Once you have selected your business name you may want to consider registering a trademark. A trademark is the ultimate protection even above the protection provided by a company name or a registered business name.

Use the URL you have purchased to create email addresses; most email service providers will allow you to use your URL in the name. Instead of having your email as fred@gmail.com or fred@bigpond.com, and so forth, you will have a much more professional looking email address such as fred@yourbusinessname.com.au. The later signals that you are not a backyard operator, that you have a website, that you have an established business and are serious about building that business, both of which are essential to presenting yourself as a successful practitioner.

Always establish a website and a Facebook page, even if both are quite basic at first. No website or Facebook page means you don't exist in today's world obsessed with electronic media, so that means in their absence you can't be trusted. Besides, some of the promotional ideas we are about to explore depend on you driving your potential customers to a website or Facebook page and having a means of contacting you on those sites.

Have it as one of your business objectives to update and refresh your website and Facebook page as your business grows and as you learn more about what image you want to project to your target market and what message you want to deliver to it.

Presentation is all important. Think about what messages you want to convey in terms of the value of the services you provide— value not cheapness. Perhaps you should consider a statement or catchphrase alongside your logo which brings to life what makes your business different. This statement can summarise an attitude, or an approach, that hopefully distinguishes your service from competitors. Make sure you consider carefully what other practitioners in your market area are doing. Visit their website, Facebook pages and Instagram listings.

Armed with your new logo, name and graphics package you should carefully consider your online presence. Traditional forms of promotion, such as placing an ad in a magazine or newspaper, have gone the way of the dodo, these days it is all about your online presence. A website is a must and again, there are a variety of options to assist you putting your website together cost effectively. Importantly, put your thoughts down on paper in detail, looking at what information you want to put out in the public domain on your site. Things to consider include your proficiency with various software accounting systems including Xero, HandiTax and MYOB, and consider how you will present your experience and professional background. Try to develop a navigation map for the home page that you would like a web developer to create for you. Once you have thought through your approach, meet with a couple of local web developers, with your written notes, and discuss how best you might be able to bring your website to reality at the most reasonable cost.

There is a variety of different software packages available, *WordPress* is a particularly good open-source option that is cheap, which you could use to do it yourself, at least initially. Some of the URL registration companies such as *GoDaddy* have their own website construction software to assist you if you wanted to do it yourself. However, those websites inevitably look home made even if they do the job initially for you. It is best to pay a developer to build the website, as well sourcing hosting services and some premium themes and plug-ins for the site, all of which will incur costs but make your site look more professional. The website is the modern-day shopfront, so you want it looking attractive. Websites depending on their complexity can take anywhere from 8-16 weeks to develop but most can be done in three months with project management along the way. Normally in setting up your business you might consider a small local ad agency that might be able to help you consolidate the design of your graphics package and website. Talk to a few and see with whom you feel comfortable.

TAP Media (at taxagentmedia.com.au) can get your website and all media requirements set up much quicker and inexpensively because they specialize in accounting practice media.

Social media, including Facebook, LinkedIn and Instagram are other tools that need to be worked on so that you develop a content plan which brings your practice to life. Presenting the progress of the development of your business can help boost local engagement. Once you have your social media presence, regularly post ideas or tips to those sites. The volume of posting boosts the visibility of your page to users. You may eventually hire a social media firm to do this for you but consistency is important, so think about your posting strategy. Consider initially posting once per week to get you going. There are several social media management software tools that can help you plan out your content each month. These can be viewed online, and you can test a few out to see which one suits you best.

Engaging with your local business community is another way you can promote your business. Often the Lions Club and local business trader groups run forums and get togethers which enable you to tap into local businesses. Think about developing a small A5 DL brochure which you can hand out to people who you are keen to engage with, outlining your services.

Make sure you develop a spreadsheet of your contacts and over time develop a database of local businesses which you can promote to, either by way of personal contact, or through being able to develop electronic direct mailers. Split your database into prospects and existing clients so that you can communicate with both on a regular basis, the former with promotional offerings and the later with technical updates to reassure your existing clients that you are trying to assist them to keep up to date with their reporting obligations and to get them the best possible tax result.

Mailchimp for example is an easy-to-use client database management and mailout system that allows large volume mailouts. High volume mailouts from your own email address runs the risk of Google thinking that you are spamming people which could lead to your email address or URL be classified by them as spam. Use a mail management provider instead. Such mail management sites also have the appropriate legal requirements for mail-outs built in including an *unsubscribe* mechanism.

Content for you to consider for both clients and prospects might include up to date accounting information, changes to tax laws, deadline reminders and other general small business news. Regularly email the database of contacts that you have developed and always use it to stay in touch with your existing clients, you need to make them feel looked after. Perhaps get a professionally prepared template to use with those Electronic Direct Mailouts (EDMs).

One of the key things to remember about acquiring accounting service clients is timing. By doing regular mailouts you will inevitably come to the small business owner's attention on the very day he or she gets disappointed by his or her current provider, at other times they're just not listening.

Developing contacts through the local football club, tennis club or using community noticeboards are another potential avenue for business prospects. Making yourself known to the local newspaper is also a good way to perhaps get some editorial on your new business.

The journey in setting up and establishing a new business requires you to keep in a mind a range of fundamentals as you consider what are the best communication avenues for your practice. A lot of the ideas discussed to this point do require expenditure of money and time but certainly the graphics package, website, good looking emails and social media are mandatory.

There are also several other guiding principles to consider as you develop your plans:

- develop a local target list of those businesses you would like to approach and prospect. The personal approach and the opportunity to meet and discuss your services is all important as you set up your business;

- make appointments and go see prospective business clients. In some cases, it may be the first time an accounting professional has ever made the effort to visit, and it signals your interest in their business. It is important that they see you and it's important that you see their business;
- develop a financial budget for your communications and allocate time each week to manage it. This should be done in conjunction with your overall business plan;
- review what is working for you and what isn't. Look at the statistics provided to you by Google and by Facebook to help fine tune your communications;
- don't be afraid to try new ideas;
- take time out to review what your competition is doing. Review their social media content. This can help you identify opportunities and gaps in their services;
- establish a personality for your business. Be professional and be human;
- put time aside for business development each week. Be adaptable and flexible. If you have a mentor who you respect and you can use as a sounding board for new ideas, make sure you have a coffee with them or catch up electronically on a regular basis;
- develop some Key Performance Indicators (KPIs) around your communication plan. Look at your website traffic stats, engagement on social media and examine any customer feedback. Make sure you fulfill your Google merchant and analytics arrangements so that you can be ahead of the game in terms of promoting your business online;

- don't be frightened to reach out to other professionals and seek help and guidance;
- understand what is out there in your local market; and
- ensure that when you communicate with the market that what you say is authentic and reflects current legal and ethical standards.

Stick at it and regularly market your business. Results will come over time.

CHAPTER FOUR

Dealing With Your Staff, Clients and Suppliers

The Australian small business market these days is demanding a full-service provider of tax, accounting and administrative services. Gone are the days when one small business had a bookkeeper and a separate Tax Agent. The inherent inefficiencies of that arrangement are obvious but mostly it was discarded because the small business owner became sick of standing in the middle of debates between their bookkeeper and their Tax Agent. The small business owner just wants to get on with conducting their business and not be distracted by issues about which they know little. In some cases, those inefficiencies and disagreements can lead to the client missing ATO deadlines or, worse still, providing inaccurate lodgements.

As their service provider, you can't be all things to all clients all the time, and you need to recognise where further more specialised advice is required and is cost effective for your client to engage. The client will expect you to know when to make that call, who to call and the cost effectiveness of getting a specialist involved. In some cases, the expense of that advice may simply outweigh any benefit the client can derive from it. This also means that you should foster a network of professionals around you that have specialised knowledge of certain tax legalities, some of whom may tolerate a casual phone call to help you to determine if more specialised work is warranted. TAP Provides a readymade network of technical support.

The client will expect you to know the basics about what the numbers mean, what form is to be used for each administrative task, when things are due and importantly, when deadlines are approaching. You need to have a basic understanding of all the governmental bodies (see Chapter Eighteen) with which your client is required to interact and what they need to do to meet those obligations. Failure to meet such obligations will inevitably be your fault even it is not strictly tax related.

You should always deal with your clients in writing other than casual conversations about the weather. If they ask a tax question, get them to put it in an email so that you know exactly what they want and, importantly, exactly what you told them. In fact, under the new ATO ethics guidelines all tax advice to your clients must be in writing and kept, with supporting information, on file for five years. That aside, you always need to have the ability to demonstrate to your client what advice was given to them about any subject and when that advice was provided. The client will want to blame you for missed deadline or inappropriate or missing advice, especially if there is a penalty involved. So, you need to be able to lay out the paperwork that demonstrates that you are not at fault.

When onboarding a client:

- have a standard onboarding checklist (see Chapter Ten) that covers all the necessary details that you need to collect from your new client;

- ensure you have identified them but you are not permitted to keep the source documents, such as copies of passports or drivers licences, that you use for that identification on file;
- after preparing a comprehensive engagement letter, get them to sign it so there is no misunderstanding about what services you are going to provide and the prices for those services. There are now certain disclosure requirements that you need to include in that letter. Obtain an up-to-date draft of such engagement letters from your professional association or from TAP;
- do your ethical letter to the previous accountant;
- obtain the directors ID if you are working with a company client;
- once they have formally engaged you, put the client on your tax portal and on your ASIC agent's register; and,
- do the ATO Client Agent Linking which is required for all entities except individual clients (but there is talk of that being brought in for individuals as well).

Always have a meeting with your client before you prepare the tax return. Talk to them about their business over the past year and changes that have occurred relevant to their tax position. It is always best to have an ATO pre-fill listing in front of you to aid that discussion, as well as a copy of last year's return. Keep notes of that discussion and keep them on file. There are computer systems available that record your meeting and turns it into a copy to send your client.

No client will expect you to know more about their business than they do. Of course, in the large corporate world there are expert consultants that get called in, at huge cost, to advise those businesses on systems or control structures or other specialised issues. That is not the case in the small business environment, you won't be expected to know more about running a butcher shop than the butcher already knows, so don't be advising him or her on how to chop things up. But you do need to know what the numbers from the business are saying to the business owner. Issues such as whether the business is over-stretched with debt, how are its costs moving against expectation, are the basic working capital ratios within expectation for the industry they are in, what does their cashflow look like and how can it be improved, should they lease or buy, are they collecting debt on time, what are their terms of trade and other key financial considerations.

In all of that, know what your limits are, especially when it comes to crossing the line into providing legal or other specialised advice. As a Tax Agent you are not licensed to provide legal advice and your client relying on such advice could mean serious trouble for you and your business. So, advice on contracts or legal disputes or conveyancing are amongst the things that are off-limits. That is also true when it comes to providing financial investment advice. It is easy to casually suggest to your client that this or that looks like a good investment, don't do that, casually or otherwise. Again, you need a financial services license to provide such advice. Stay in your lane, know what you are legally intitled to do and stay out of trouble.

Don't offer credit to your clients. For larger jobs take 50% upfront and get the rest before you lodge the return, let me emphasise *payment before lodgement*. If the job is small enough for you to knock it over quickly, then do it and then issue the invoice but, again, get paid before you lodge the return. You have no leverage to collect the debt once you lodge the return. Resist the inclination to believe that this or that client is *reliable*. When it comes to money no one is reliable. Especially resist the temptation to offer credit to your friends, they will understand that you have a business to run. Small business clients often are not impressed by you offering credit, in fact they are more likely to think that you are an idiot. In fact, you should be advising them to avoid offering credit. Don't get fooled by the notion that your client will eventually have to come back to you when their next BAS is due so you will have leverage to get paid then. There are two problems with that notion: firstly, ask yourself will they in fact come back, the fact that they don't want to pay you may cause them to leave; and secondly, do you want your debtors to be constantly more than 90 days overdue.

Offering credit is the single biggest killer of small business and accounting practices. That is right up there with under-pricing your work and not paying the ATO on time.

On occasion your client may want you to sign what is often called an *accountant's letter* for a lender from whom the client is seeking finance. The name and form of the letter sound deliberately innocuous. Be very careful of such letters. The lender often deliberately looks to place the onus on the accountant to *certify the profitability* of the client's business operations. You are not an auditor; you only work on the figures and facts provided to you by your clients. You can confirm to the lender that you are their accountant, and whether the client is up to date with their tax lodgements but that is about it. Clauses in such letters like *I understand the Lender is relying on this certification letter when assessing the making of the loan* are very dangerous and expose you to liability.

Don't let fees for a particular client just drift upward without, inflation aside, providing a commensurate increase in the value you provide to them. Importantly, the same applies to your own service providers. All product and service providers treat new customers better than they treat loyal customers, so be new, not loyal. Regularly tender all your service providers including, phones, banks and insurance. When tendering, develop a detailed brief to the service provider of what your requirements are so that there is no misunderstanding regarding what you want to buy. Regularly review those requirements looking for internal efficiencies.

Staffing is a whole other bag of worms, fraught with pitfalls. Firstly, always do contracts for employees including non-compete obligations and clearly spelling out pay rates, work and leave entitlements, job objectives and a clear description of the work they are responsible for providing and, last but not least, termination rules and termination pay. Get your lawyer to look over your draft employment contract.

Secondly, resist putting on staff for as long as you can when starting out within the constraint of the resource requirements to properly service your clients.

Thirdly, your first hire should be a bookkeeper not an accountant or receptionist. You will, when you start out, probably use a contract bookkeeper for work you can't do yourself. But bring that task inhouse as soon as you can for reasons of cost management and quality control and they can then be used to provide educated cover for you when you are not available.

You need personally to give up the bookkeeping as soon as you can to focus on tax work and client service provision because bookkeeping pay rates are less than what you need to be paid.

Your next hire after that first bookkeeper probably should also be another bookkeeper, preferably with a BAS agents license, and then after that the junior administrator or receptionist to make up a four-person practice. That staffing should get you close to a one million dollar turnover. We'll cover this off more completely in the next chapter but a good rule of thumb in calculating your turnover should be at least four times your gross wages including super and a reasonable wage for the principal.

A few cautionary tales. The non-compete clauses in your employment contracts are, in Australia, pretty much useless, but put them in anyway. The Trade Practices Act prevents you from restricting a person's ability to ply their trade. The Act trumps your contract. For this reason, you should think long and hard about bringing a fully qualified Tax Agent, or near Tax Agent qualified, person into your practice. It is a sad indictment of some people starting out in the profession that they will use your practice to get to know your clients, then leave to start their own practice and take your clients with them. I am not saying that it is impossible to find the right person, I'm just saying be careful.

Be very clear about what you expect from your staff and put it in writing. Review those objectives regularly. Again, in Australia, it is difficult to fire staff. You need to follow the protocol of warnings before you fire them. That is a reason why you need to put termination conditions, including how much notice they will receive, in their employment contract. Familiarise yourself with industry standards in your state.

Hire only good people. That sounds obvious but it is difficult to get right. When you bring someone on be cognisant of the office culture, the last thing you want is in-office conflict—that is both a huge loss generator and devalues the work environment.

Set clear standards for your staff for ethical and honest behaviour and be the example that they follow. It is probably worthwhile to have someone designated in your office to keep an eye out for ATO legislative changes. Have a weekly meeting to discuss as a group the technical issues and administrative problems that arise during any given week.

CHAPTER FIVE

What Size Practice Do I Want;
Mergers and Acquisitions

In the previous chapter we talked about building your practice to a turnover of around one million dollars. You don't have to grow that large. Perhaps you would consider a practice made up of just you and perhaps some bookkeeping support adequate for your needs. Just keep in mind that you need to be able to adequately service your clients and keep abreast of all tax law developments. The same rule of thumb for calculating your expected turnover applies in a smaller practice, four times your gross wages including you.

There are several small tax practices out there that are doing a fine job servicing their clients. They typically have decided not to grow beyond just themselves because of concerns related to employing staff, some of which we have already covered, or it just fits their personal lifestyle. Keep in mind as a single person practice that you should develop networks that allow you to keep in touch with the profession and that allow you to provide specialised advice that ensures your client is paying the correct amount of tax.

Growing past the four-person practice noted in the previous chapter brings issues. If you wanted to grow beyond that size the next logical step would be to add a third bookkeeper BAS Agent, making three bookkeepers, you and a junior administration assistant who also helps with social media and regular contact with your prospect list and a newsletter for your existing clients. That would allow you to grow past a one-million-dollar turnover. But with growth comes the obstacle of keeping up with service levels needed by your clients. That means inevitably that you are adding that next staff member ahead of the sales revenues needed to fully utilise that added resource. So, it is stepwise growth, with an increase in costs followed by an increase in sales. To do it the other way round risks alienating your existing client base by underservicing their needs.

As previously mentioned, you need to be careful if you are considering the addition of another fully qualified Tax Agent/ accountant because of the risk of them leaving with some of your clients. No, a non-compete arrangement will *not* stop them from stealing your clients. That is not to say that employing a fully qualified person can't work, there are many such arrangements that are successful, and there is the issue of the benefit in mentoring young professionals. I am just saying be careful who you choose.

That is also true, perhaps even doubly true, if you acquire another practice which includes an existing fully qualified staff member that you are expected to employ for the sake of *continuity* after you buy the practice but who are not a legal participant in the purchase contract. I make the distinction about being part of the purchase contract because non-compete arrangements have a good chance of sticking where you have paid money to acquire a business as opposed to simply trying to stop an employee from practicing.

Buying another practice is a difficult proposition and you inevitably come up against the risk of clients leaving because the previous owner is no longer there or has retired. A retiring owner is the best scenario, an owner going off to *do other things* opens the possibility that they will simply set up elsewhere, far enough away so as not to breach the non-compete clauses in the purchase contract. Remember *far enough away* in the electronic age where most work is being done over the internet probably makes territorial-based no compete clauses meaningless. You are not going to be able to enforce a non-compete clause that says that the previous owner can't compete anywhere in Australia. It is difficult to stop the previous owner from practicing, in fact the Trade Practices Act says that you can't stop them. Your acquisition contract can have all sorts of non-compete clauses but in the end, they are entitled to practice elsewhere. A court would expect the seller to abide by the contract within the constraints of the Trade Practices Act. But, as with all things in business, going to court is an expensive exercise and almost always leads to a dead loss whichever way the ruling goes.

From a professional standards point of view, the exiting owner should recognise that they sold the clients to you. But keep in mind the previous owner is entitled, *as a courtesy*, to let the clients you purchased know that he or she has left and in so doing, provide them with his or her future contact details. Your position where the clients you purchased chase the previous owner is much weaker compared to a situation where you can prove the exiting owner is promoting himself or herself to your new practice's clients.

The other side of the acquisition transaction is the clients themselves. They are not the chattels of the previous owner, they can't physically be bought or sold. They will decide for themselves whether they stay or go, and most will take the opportunity to tender their accounting services when a practice sale has taken place. So, it is going to come down to how well the handover is managed. You can, and must, mitigate the loss of clients by immediately meeting with all key clients and allowing them to see your worth as an accountant. The risk of losing clients decreases with the size of the practice you are acquiring because the clients can see that most of the staff of the target practice are staying. But that brings with it the exposure previously outlined. If one or two of those staff that stay are qualified or near qualified Tax Agents, then the practice being sold is an ideal excuse for them to leave and set up on their own.

I am not saying that acquiring a practice can't work. It happens regularly to varying degrees of success. The key thing you can do is insist on *holdback* of a proportion of the purchase price, as large a holdback as you can negotiate, with the remainder of the purchase price being payable after one full (audited) trading year so that you and the existing owner can see how many clients you actually purchased. You need to consult a lawyer in constructing such arrangements. Beyond that, do your due diligence, go through the books and client arrangements of the target practice with a fine-tooth combe and be very active managing the handover.

During the handover period, say one year, do not change pricing or the service standards and conditions enjoyed by the clients under the previous owner even if you think those matters need to change. The exception being if you can increase the *value add* for your new clients without increasing the price offered. Let the sale settle down before you act on price. In fact, you changing prices, or service levels, is an excuse for the previous owner to demand full payment of the holdback monies blaming you for losing any clients who left the practice.

The other way to grow is by merging with another firm. The merger can be with a larger or smaller firm and whether it is suitable for you would depend on the terms that you can negotiate in either case. Those terms should include the salaries of the principals of the combined practice, the authority levels of each principal, the mechanisms related to decision making going forward, the dividend policy and the exit or demerger or practice sale conditions. The key consideration with mergers is your compatibility with the other principal or principals. Having a partner or partners brings with it certain challenges that you need to be prepared for, not unlike a marriage, and those issues all have a lot to do with the compatibility of the people involved including, perhaps first and foremost, a shared vision of where you, as a group, want to take the combined practice.

CHAPTER SIX

The Australian Tax Office (ATO)

This text does not attempt to be a tax manual. Income tax law is constantly changing but the subject matter of this manual has a longer shelf life. If you wish to look up current tax law on a particular subject seek out current information from the ATO or the many fine publications covering current tax law or join one of the approved professional bodies and take advantage of their technical resources and seminars. TAP also provides support in this regard.

On that very subject a Tax Agent is required to keep up to date with changes in the law. You need to ensure that you keep your professional development hours at least in line with the Tax Practitioners Board's guidelines for Tax Agents.

Generally speaking the ATO is your friend. They primarily want to ensure that taxpayers are compliant with the law and that returns submitted are correct. By *correct* I mean that the taxpayer has neither been overtaxed nor has paid less tax than they are required to pay. The ATO will cooperate with you to assist any client to get it right and assist with payment plans if the client can't immediately meet their payment obligations. Use the resources they provide and work with them to resolve any issues on a timely basis. If it becomes clear that the client is avoiding their responsibilities, the ATO can be quite formidable if the client is not meeting their obligations and if there are indications of evasion, then the good will that exists between the client and the ATO disappears.

It is not worthwhile for you to work with any client who exhibits a willingness to evade tax. Such clients will cost you time and money but most importantly they threaten your own reputation with the tax office. Drop them as soon as it is clear that they don't want to do the right thing.

The ATO has a mixed history when it comes to a Tax Agent dobbing tax evading clients in because of considerations of confidentiality but recent ethical guidelines seem to favour you reporting the client. Frankly, it is best simply to get rid of them before you come into possession of any clear evidence of tax evasion.

One of the attributes of clients who continually move or shop their tax services, the cheap clients, is that they may be moving accountants because the accountant is refusing to help them avoid tax rather than the client being, by nature, cheap. Always ensure you exchange ethical letters with any new client's previous accountant. But that doesn't necessarily mean that their previous accountant is going to alert you to any suspicious behaviour because of confidentiality requirements. It does mean that you are wasting your time pursuing cheap or transient clients because they have no loyalty, they are always more demanding than clients who pay reasonable fees and they may be moving their business around between accountants because they are trying to hide their intentions regarding tax evasion as opposed to them being cost averse. You will never get a decent return on your investment with them, and they may get you into trouble. Regardless of why a client is cheap they are best avoided.

The ATO needs to consider legislation that protects agents who uncover fraud. Until that happens stay in your lane. One has to hope with any such legislation that they don't turn us all into unpaid tax auditors.

Such matters are sadly never black and white. Follow your gut and the law. You don't want to get caught up with tax evaders when inevitably the ATO comes calling. I have had a situation where I refused a client and refused to tell the client's new agent why I refused to service the client, and the new agent diligently refused to act for that client because of what I *wasn't* saying rather than what I told him. I received threatening letters from the client because he presupposed that I had warned the new accountant off, which in itself is highly suspicious behavior for the client to exhibit. But I didn't say a word, the new accountant had intuited my reluctance to answer any of his questions and was prudently wary of any such entanglements. I would strongly suggest that you as a Tax Agent be equally careful of such matters when taking on a client. There was no follow through from the discarded client, probably because he didn't want the attention. The ATO leaves us out on a limb in this area. No fee is worth getting caught up in that nightmare.

Uncovering concrete evidence of fraud is a different matter. You have obligations. Deal with such matters through a lawyer, and stay anonymous until your lawyer tells you that you are fully indemnified. You do not want to be in a position where it can be shown you had concrete evidence of tax fraud and did nothing even though the ATO leaves you susceptible to be eaten. The ATO attitudes toward reporting fraud are currently changing, so stay abreast of your ethical responsibilities. The current position of the ATO can be summarised as the obligations in sections 30-35 and 30-40 of the TASA which applies to a significant breach of the Code where a registered tax practitioner has reasonable grounds to believe that the breach occurred on or after 1 July 2024.

More generally, respond quickly and comprehensively to all ATO requests. I have only ever found them to be helpful. They are not combative unless the client forces them to be. Typically, like you and any decent client, they just want to get it right. They are definitely not looking to have your client pay more tax than they have to pay but they equally are not going to perform the function of legally minimising the tax your client has to pay, that's your job. They will work with you and your client on any issue including your client's difficulty in paying any tax debt. They have some smart people working with them if the issue gets down to the very fine points of the law. Always be open and transparent with them. If your client has dug a hole for themselves then get the ATO involved early and outline the circumstances that the client finds themselves in. Declaration of the problem early is always your best choice. The ATO will help and they will negotiate payment arrangements suitable to your client's circumstances.

If there is a problem, ensure your client doesn't stick their head in the sand. That is the worst choice leading to the worst outcome. If the ATO uncovers the problem themselves on audit both you and your client may find yourselves dealing with their legal people. Their legal people have a different set of priorities, and a different performance risk profile in regard to protecting their own jobs.

They will, appropriately, take the hard, by the book, line. You do not want to put your client in a position where they are dealing with the ATO through their legal people or, worse still, through the courts. Court action against the ATO is expensive, usually more expensive than any prospective gain, and often futile. Having asserted that, if your client has deep pockets and a decent prospect of winning it can be useful to test certain parts of the tax act, just wear a helmet.

CHAPTER SEVEN

Debits and Credits and
the Reconciliation of Financial Accounts

The first known documentation of the double-entry accounting system was recorded in 1494 by Luca Pacioli, who is widely known today as the 'father of accounting' because of the book he published that year detailing the concepts of the double-entry bookkeeping method, Summa di Arithmetica Geometria Proportioni and Proportionalita. You should have a translated edition of that book in your personal library. He was also called Luca di Borgo after his birthplace, Borgo Sansepolcro, in Tuscany. Just like Newtons hypothesis that for every action there is an equal and opposite reaction, Pacioli posited that for every transaction into a business there is a transaction out. He proposed the three golden rules of accounting: 1) Debit what comes in and credit what goes out; 2) Credit the giver and debit the receiver; and 3) Credit all income and debit all expenses. Basically, if money goes in it must come from somewhere, if money goes out it must go somewhere. The logic is inescapable. If the total of those transactions doesn't balance, then any differences need to be explained.

Using this method the purpose of bookkeeping becomes to maintain a systematic record of financial activities and transactions recorded chronologically. The purpose of accounting more generally is to report the financial strength of an entity and obtain the results of the operating activity of that business primarily by using that bookkeeping information.

To be a decent Tax Agent you must understand that method. Without a competent understanding of bookkeeping, you have no chance of understanding the source and meaning of the numbers being generated by your client's accounting system. It is essential that you understand both those things when entering numbers into a tax return or, quite simply, you will get the tax return wrong.

I've been through university, including postgraduate, and a lot of university-trained accounting students come through with little idea of how bookkeeping works. By that I mean how to post business transactions to a ledger, how to reconcile a ledger, how to produce a set of financial statements, how a director's loan account works, how shareholder's equity works, how all that relates to taxable revenue, how to manage a franking account and how to verify the figures in a balance sheet. That information is critical for preparing an accurate tax return. The first thing you should do if you want to have a successful tax practice is to go get a Certificate IV in bookkeeping, or equivalent course, from an ATO accredited tertiary institution.

The all-important *accounting equation* becomes the formula that shows that the sum of a company's liabilities and shareholders' equity are equal to its total assets, that is assets = liabilities + equity. That clear-cut relationship between a company's liabilities, assets and equity is the backbone to double-entry bookkeeping. The result of a company's accounting equation is numbers in its balance sheet and profit and loss (P&L) statement. Equity can be shareholders' equity, stockholders' equity, or owner's equity or loans and, as the balance sheet name implies, the ledger being *kept* must balance. If it does balance, it is one of the few things in life where you can be sure that you have the right answer.

Like other equations, if two terms of the basic accounting equation are known, you can solve for the third term. For example, total assets – total liabilities = total equity, or total assets – total equity = total liabilities. You move a term from the right side to the left side of the accounting equation by using a minus sign. Names meaning the same as balance sheet are: Statement of Financial Position or Statement of Financial Condition.

Equity is named owner's equity, shareholders' equity, or stockholders' equity on the balance sheet. Business owners with a sole proprietorship and small businesses that aren't corporations use owner's equity. Corporations with shareholders may call equity either shareholders' equity or stockholders' equity.

In double-entry accounting or bookkeeping, total debits on the left side must equal total credits on the right side (in the old days which side of the paper ledgers mattered). That's the case for each business transaction and the journal entry should have both parts of that one transaction. As a result, the financial statements are in balance. The monthly *trial balance* is a listing of account names from the chart of accounts with total account balances or amounts. Total debits and credits must be equal before posting transactions to the general ledger for the accounting cycle. Accounting software systems are all based on double-entry accounting that automatically generating the trial balance. The trial balance includes columns with total debit and total credit transactions at the bottom of the report.

41

The accounting can be done either on a cash basis or an accrual basis. A cash basis, as the name implies, means that transactions are accounted for on the date they move from or into the bank account and only if they create movement in the bank account within the period being measured. An accrual basis means that certain income and costs are accounted for ahead of time providing the bookkeeper has a good faith, well documented reason, for bringing them to account. An example of an accrual transaction would be known upcoming salary related commitments.

Most small businesses use a cash basis. It is important to note that if the Business Activity Statement, the BAS, has been prepared on a cash basis then the tax returns should also be prepared on a cash basis, and vice versa. You can't move from one method to the other each year or each quarter depending on what gives you a better result because year on year, and quarter on quarter, comparisons then become meaningless. Also, there is a lot of work to do to make that change, and, importantly, the ATO doesn't allow you to flip between methods. Pick a method and stick with it. You can change it but, basically, only once. You are required to declare whether you are using cash or accrual on BAS and tax statements.

When doing the bookkeeping don't suspend transactions, that is, put them in a balance sheet item called *suspense*. Suspending items is lazy bookkeeping and simply means you couldn't be bothered to go and find out what was the actual nature of that transaction. Suspended items don't make it to the Profit and Loss (P&L) Statement or the tax return. If you encounter suspended items in a set of accounts when doing the tax return, you need to list off the transactions in the suspense account and get answers as to what the nature of them are, and the support for those transactions and, if possible, have the bookkeeper clear the suspense account out.

Making a *provision* is only available if you are using accrual accounting. A provision is the inclusion of income or expenses that have not yet hit the bank account. These do have an impact on the P&L and the tax return. So, when doing the tax return, you need to have a good long look at the basis for those provisions and reconcile those provisions to determine their validity.

Just recapping, in double-entry accounting, debits (dr) record all of the money flowing *into* an account. So, if your business were to take out a $5,000 small business loan, the cash you receive from that loan would be recorded as a debit in your cash, or assets, bank account. Credits (cr) record money that flows *out* of an account. To use that same example from above, if you received that $5,000 loan, you would record a credit of $5,000 in your liabilities account.

For example, at the risk of being overly simplistic:

- one account might represent all of the cash your client has in their business bank account (the 'cash' account);
- another account might represent the total value of all the furniture the business has in its office (the 'furniture' account); and
- another account might represent a bank loan they recently took out (the 'bank loan' account).

Here is what buying a desk for $600 would look like using an accounting system. You credit your cash account, because money is flowing out of it. Your 'furniture' account, which represents the total value of all the furniture your company owns, also changes, in this case, it increases by $600 (the value of the desk). You debit your furniture account, because value is flowing into it (a desk). In double-entry accounting, every debit (inflow) always has a corresponding credit (outflow). So, we record them together in one entry. An accountant would say that we are *crediting* the bank account $600 and *debiting* the furniture account $600.

How debits and credits affect liability accounts is straight forward. The two accounts used in the above example, cash and furniture are both asset accounts. That is, they keep track of something the business *owns*. But not all accounts are asset accounts. Some accounts keep track of what you owe, liabilities, and other accounts keep track of the total value of your business, equity. If the business takes out a $1,000 bank loan, and that increases, debits, the cash account by $1,000. In addition to adding $1,000 to your cash account, it would also have to increase the liability account by $1,000 because the 'bank loan account' measures not how much the business has but how much the business owes. The more the business owes, the larger the value in the bank loan account is going to be. In this case, we're crediting an account but the value of the account is increasing. That's because the account keeps track of a debt, and the debt is going *up* in this case. How debits and credits affect equity accounts is also straight forward. Why is it that crediting an equity account makes it go up, rather than down? That's because equity accounts don't measure how much the business has, rather, they measure all the claims that *investors* have against the business.

The general ledger stores business transactions organised by account and by date. Reconciling the general ledger ensures the business has correctly recorded each transaction by comparing source documents such as statements, cheques and invoices, with the accounting records. Please refer to a later explanation of the reconciliation process.

Before accounting software existed, businesses would record every business transaction in a 'general journal', a chronological transaction log. The same transaction gets written down in another book called the 'general ledger', which keeps a running balance of every account. It is fair to say that the advent of computerised accounting systems, whilst labour saving, has made some Tax Agents lazy when it comes to not only verifying figures but also understanding the figures.

Single-entry bookkeeping is a cash system, usually using excel spreadsheets which simply records incoming and outgoing cash in a single listing. It is not used by professional accountants or bookkeepers, and you will only come across it in a small business where the owner is doing the books on his or her kitchen table. If you do encounter it then it means you have a lot of work to do to reproduce the bank reconciliations and to make sure the whole thing balances so, take that into account when you are quoting the price for your services to your client.

The general journal and general ledger still exist in the modern era of accounting, just not in an analogue format. Instead of recording each transaction in two places, the system records transactions once, reducing the likelihood of transposition errors. A general ledger reconciliation looks different, and is easier, thanks to the advent of accounting software. Your client's business should still conduct general ledger reconciliations at least quarterly to catch errors in transaction amounts and categories. Technology is not immune to mistakes.

This is how you prepare a general ledger reconciliation:

1. Compare beginning and ending account balances.

Before you begin the deep dive into the business's transactions, verify that asset, liability and equity accounts' prior period ending balances equal this period's beginning balances, down to the cent. If the business uses accounting software, you'll be able to complete this step quickly. Temporary accounts, revenues and expenses, start at zero at the beginning of every period. Accounting software can automatically prepare closing entries at the end of each accounting period, zeroing out revenues and expenses for a fresh start in the upcoming period. *Close* the books at least annually but it's best practice to do it monthly. Those businesses who keep their books manually should take their time in this step. They don't want to be wracking their brains later trying to find what turns out to be a senseless opening error.

To compare beginning and ending account balances, look at the company's adjusted trial balance from the previous accounting period and the general ledger from this accounting period. For asset, liability and equity accounts, match the ending balance on the trial balance to the general ledger's beginning balance. Revenue and expense accounts should start with a zero balance. Compare the ending trial balance and the opening general ledger balance for each account.

2. Reconcile accounts to the general ledger. Account by account, comb through all the transactions listed on the general ledger for the period. Make sure it has documentation supporting the date, dollar amount and accounts involved. The bank account is probably the most active, meaning it'll take the longest to reconcile. Most accounting software packages have a bank

reconciliation feature that automates part of the process. If the owner is not the only person with access to the business funds, you should match approval documentation to each transaction. After you've reconciled the cash accounts, you can move onto your other, smaller accounts. Manual bookkeepers need to add an extra step here. Since you store transactions in the general journal and the general ledger, there's a chance you're missing a transaction in one place. Create a column in the books to place a checkmark when transactions in the general ledger and general journal match. You should also recalculate each account total to weed out clerical errors.

To complete the reconciliation, pull up the company's invoice, which corroborates the transaction's date and amount.

Ensure that you have verified the asset and liability balances. Fixed assets should be supported by an asset listing. Understand and reconcile how this feeds through into the calculation of the depreciation shown in the books.

Take the time to get a copy of at least the major lease agreements and loan agreements and ensure the asset, the liability and the interest costs are properly reflected in the accounts.

3. Create correcting entries:

So, you completed an account reconciliation and noticed an amount was entered incorrectly. You can fix it with a correcting entry. It's best practice not to edit an incorrect entry. Instead, record a correcting entry. You can either reverse the erroneous transaction and create a new entry or, you can create a new entry that fixes the error in one fell swoop. You're less likely to make another error if you try the former method. Besides correcting errors by creating new journals leaves a clearer audit trail.

4. Prepare adjusting entries:

It's customary to record depreciation and other adjusting entries at the end of the accounting period, after you're sure there are no errors in the books. The accounting software can automatically generate recurring journal entries when it's appropriate. Adjusting entries for accrued expenses and deferred revenue must eventually be reversed to avoid misstating the business's financial position.

5. Run reports:

Now that you're confident in the accuracy of the account balances, you can generate the basic financial statements to analyse the general ledger transactions. In essence, you just conducted an income statement and balance sheet reconciliation. When you use accounting software to draft financial statements, you shouldn't have to do another GL account reconciliation until next month.

Take the time to understand the figures. Consider whether the figures 'look right' and form a view for yourself whether you are prepared to accept these figures. Comparing year-on-year balances can assist with this task. Don't be afraid to send a list of concerns you may have back to the bookkeeper or the client and have them explain why the figures are what they are before you use them to prepare the tax return. This process is not just good practice—it is compulsory. The ATO expects you to *diligently* go over the financials.

A director's loan is a unique financing option but many business owners aren't aware of the potential risks and obligations associated with them or the proper accounting methodology for them. If you are a director or owner of a company, you're entitled to take loans from the company you own. A director's loan, or a shareholder's loan, is a financing option that is often taken advantage of by business owners. Director's loans are very different from personal loans, with many specific tax implications and restrictions that must be understood. If you're aware of the complex details regarding director's loans and the business is operating with a well-organised accounting strategy, director's loans can be a good financing option. A director's loan isn't simply an interest-free loan, although many businessowners make the mistake of viewing it as such. It's important to understand the tax implications and other specifics of director's loans. As a specialised financing case, director's loans present ample opportunities to make mistakes, here's what you need to know.

Put simply, a director's loan is money borrowed from a company by the company director. If a company director, a shareholder, or someone affiliated with a shareholder, takes money out of the company that isn't a dividend or wages or drawings (all of which appear in the recipient's tax return), then it means that they are borrowing company money. The nature of a director's loan or shareholder's loan doesn't change whether they take the money out of the company in a single lump sum, or over several instances. In either case, taking money out of a company in this manner is a loan and likely falls under Division 7A of the Income Tax Assessment Act 1936, which means, in most cases that the loan could be subject to tax. A borrower taking money from a company in this manner is not likely taxed on the capital removed if the loan is not a payment. If the money taken from the company is defined as a payment under Division 7A purposes, it's likely that the fringe benefits tax will be applied, which is also referred to as a benefit in kind. In this specific case, Division 7A doesn't apply to the loan amount. For example, a director and sole shareholder of a company may decide to use a company car. The provision of an asset to an employee, under the terms of Division 7A, is a payment. As an employee of the company, the director also received a loan on an interest-free basis from the company, this loan is also recognised under Division 7A.

The private use of the company car in this example is a fringe benefit, rather than a dividend. The car remains an asset of the business but its private use is subject to fringe benefits tax. The client must have a log book that verifies the percentage of private use of the vehicle.

The director or shareholder of a company must track all money in a director's loan account. The amount of the loan interest should also be recorded in the personal assessment tax return of the director or shareholder and in the company books as income.

The absence of a regularly updated Div7a loan agreement or where the obligations of that agreement are not complied with by the borrower will mean, on audit, that the full amount of the loan principle will be deemed income in the hands of the borrower. If the total amount of the borrowing was deemed to be income in the hands or the owner or borrower because they hadn't complied with the div7a requirements, or worse, still didn't have an agreement in place, would represent a serious financial challenge for the responsible person. You will, of course, be responsible for the mishap.

Director's loans can cause difficult problems in a business when they are taken for reasons unrelated to the company itself, such as increasing the salary of a director. Director's loans often start small but rapidly increase in size, because they are fed by shareholders or directors drawing capital from a business. In many cases, there is little to no oversight over these transactions other than by the person borrowing the capital. Under Division 7A, any shareholder or director's loans should be established through a formal loan agreement that details repayment terms and interest charges. Not following this procedure can cause significant problems. Director's loans can also raise red flags with the ATO when disclosed in company tax returns, if a director's loan is not administered through a proper loan agreement with relevant documentation, you may be taxed on the entire loan amount.

Lastly, director's loans may reflect poorly on the overall financial health of a business if not administered and managed correctly, creating obstacles when a business owner chooses to sell their business or brings in employee shareholders or takes a partner or seeks finance. Borrowing company capital can be a strategic move in specific, limited circumstances, especially in restrictive lending markets. There are a number of other scenarios in which a director's or shareholder's loan can be the right choice. A company may have surplus cash which is not immediately required for normal operational requirements. In this case, a loan that represents only a small percentage of overall company assets, such as less than 10 percent, may be an effective finance option.

Director's or shareholder's loans should not be used to solve short term cash flow problems. Borrowing company funds to fund life style expenses, for personal cash or bills, or because your wage as a director is not sufficient, is likely to disrupt the financial health of your business. Borrowing money from your company through a director's or shareholder's loan is relatively straightforward but requires approval from shareholders. If the business is a sole proprietorship, this approval is not implied, they'll need to keep a copy of the written approval on file. The loan agreement you use to administer the loan must be in force before the lodgement date of the company year income in order to be compliant with Division 7A. The minimum yearly repayments on director's and shareholder's loans fall under Division 7a. If the minimum repayment on a director's loan is not made, the deficient amount becomes a dividend in that financial year under Division 7A rules. These repayments and interest charges must be shown in the general ledger as actual money changing hands. Borrowers must make the minimum repayment amount before June 30th in the year in which they are due. The calculation of the minimum repayment amount is performed on the basis of the total loans made to a shareholder or director.

Overall, a director's loan is intended to function as a short-term loan to cover expenses related to the operational costs of a business and should be treated accordingly. Administering a director's loan in a compliant manner can be a complicated process.

One of the things that is poorly accounted for in company books is the franking account. This area is often misunderstood and poorly administered. Failure to properly keep track of franking credits means your client may overpay tax. A franking account records the amount of tax paid that a franking entity can pass on to its members or shareholders as a franking credit. Each entity that is, or has ever been, a corporate tax entity has a franking account. An entity is considered a *franking entity* if it is a corporate tax entity. A corporate tax entity includes a company, corporate limited partnership, corporate unit trust, or public trading trust but does not include a mutual life insurance company or a company acting in its capacity as trustee of a trust.

A franking credit is most commonly recorded in the account if the entity receives a franked distribution, pays income tax or a PAYG instalment, or incurs a liability for franking deficit tax (FDT). The credit is equal to the amount of tax or PAYG instalment paid, the franking credit attached to the distribution received, or the FDT liability incurred. In other words, the credit is equal to the amount of tax paid. Where an income tax liability is only partially paid, franking credits will not arise for the amount that remains outstanding. Partial payments made towards outstanding activity statement liabilities will be allocated in accordance with the ATO policies. Franking credits will only arise to the extent that a partial payment is allocated towards a PAYG Instalment liability.

A franked distribution is an arrangement in Australia that eliminates the double taxation on dividends. The shareholder can reduce the tax paid on the dividend paid to them by the franking entity by an amount equal to the tax imputation credits. Franking deficit tax is the basic principle that an entity must not give its members credit for more tax than what has actually been paid. As such the FDT rules require an entity to reconcile its franking account at certain times. An entity will have to pay FDT when the account is in deficit.

A franking debit is most commonly recorded in the franking account if the entity pays a franked distribution to its members or receives a refund of income tax. The franking debit is equal to the franking credit attached to the distribution or the amount of tax refunded.

A franking account is a rolling balance account, this means the balance of the account rolls over from one income year to another. At any time, the franking account can be either in surplus or deficit. The account is in surplus if the amount of franking credits in the account is more than the sum of franking debits. The account is in deficit if the number of franking debits exceeds the amount of franking credits.

For a profitable company generating surplus cashflow a director may withdraw a small wage or director's fee. Having tax minimisation in mind, directors may withdraw further amounts from the company's cash resources. These additional withdrawals will not appear as a wage or directors fee expense in the profit and loss report but as a company asset in the form of a Directors Loan Account appearing on its balance sheet. To avoid Division 7A implications and remove a debit director's loan one option is increasing the wage being paid to the directors and have the company remit PAYG withholding to the ATO or pay a director's fee. Alternatively, if the directors are also shareholders, which is often the case, the company can declare a dividend. Depending on the company's tax circumstances, shareholders might enjoy the benefit of a franked dividend where the tax credits paid by the company are transferred to them in paying a fully franked dividend. If the company does not have accumulated profits, then a dividend cannot be paid. These equity and loan accounts need to be reconciled at least yearly, preferably quarterly.

General ledger reconciliations fall into three categories: assets, liabilities, or equity. Each general ledger reconciliation corresponds to a balance sheet account, having the same GL account number and name. Companies have varying general ledger reconciliations, but many are standard, including:

- bank reconciliation: a bank reconciliation is done for each bank account to reconcile the company's GL balance to the bank statement. It's normal for bank recs to have reconciling items because of timing differences, like outstanding checks, bank service fees, or pending deposits;

- accounts receivable reconciliation: this rec ties the A/R balance to the sub-ledger, called the A/R Aging Report, to ensure all customer invoices, payments and credit memos are captured on time and accurately;
- fixed assets reconciliation: this rec ties property, equipment, furniture and depreciation balances to the fixed assets subledger. The fixed asset sub-ledger tracks the acquisition, depreciation, transfer and disposal of fixed assets. If the asset register is sizable, it may warrant physical verification by sighting and potentially bringing the assets back to market value;
- accounts payable reconciliation: this rec ties the GL balance to the AP sub-ledger, the AP Aging Report, to accurately capture money owed and paid to suppliers;
- payroll reconciliation: this can be one consolidated rec or broken out by Salaries & Wages, Payroll Taxes, 401K, Medical and others. This account reconciliation ensures payroll-related expenses and liabilities are recorded in a way that's consistent with payroll reports;
- debt reconciliations: these general ledger reconciliations specify long-term amounts owed to others (i.e. notes, mortgage, interest payable) and tie debt balances in the general ledger to creditors' account statements; and
- equity reconciliations: this is where the owners' net worth is agreed to accumulated income or deficits. The equity reconciliations are where the company's net income (or loss) is closed from the income statement which includes operating income, gains & losses and dividends. It will also include other equity items such as owner capital investments and share-based compensation expenses.

Performing the reconciliations involves several steps:

1. Identify accounts: first, run a trial balance to ensure all balance sheet accounts are captured. Run this each time you reconcile accounts in case new GL accounts were added since the last time you reconciled.
2. Compare balances: match the book (also called GL) balance to the sub-ledger or independent source balance. A sub-ledger could be an AR aging or prepaid expense schedule, while a bank statement is an independent source document.
3. Investigate discrepancies: if the GL and independent source balances don't match, the reconciler must identify the reason(s) for the variance.
4. Identify reconciling items: itemise reconciling items including the date, description and corrective action to take to resolve.
5. Review and approve: after the reconciler completes these steps, the account reviewer will confirm the reconciler's analysis and either send it back to the reconciler for additional work or sign off to confirm the account's activity as accurate.

Accountants perform general ledger reconciliations each accounting period, usually monthly, quarterly, or annually. Typically, accounts are reconciled monthly, but the frequency varies depending on factors like transaction volume or management's assessment of risk for that specific account. Bank accounts that receive customer payments can be reconciled daily due to high volume, while an interest payable account gets reconciled quarterly because there's only a few transactions posted each month.

The volume of transactions that flows through a business each period can be overwhelming to track manually. With Excel, managing a large amount of data becomes burdensome and increases the risk of errors and typos. Automating the general ledger reconciliation process minimizes the risk of these errors while making reconciling accounts a more efficient process.

CHAPTER EIGHT

Working Papers

The ATO requires that you keep your working papers, including any written tax advice with the supporting documents, for a minimum of five years.

Here is a brief overview of what working papers you should keep and how you should arrange them for each client.

Starting with work paper file notes, these are important for several reasons:

1. They confirm how the figures in the financial statements are verified.
2. During the process of completing the work papers for each section, the accountant gains an insight as to how the client's business is trading. Is the bookkeeping reliable or have shortcuts been done? Is the business viable?
3. Once the financial statements and tax returns have been completed, it is good practice to then set aside some independent time to review the job as a 'reviewer', not as the preparing accountant.

4. Work papers and file notes are key evidence in supporting your work. The ATO will, on audit, require you to verify and support your work. Professional bodies may audit your work if you become subject to a practice quality review. They cannot rely on your memory. They will audit the paper trail. Your insurance also will rely on the quality of your work papers. Attach your research if required. Your client will rely on the advice you have provided. Back yourself, ensure you have great substantiated work papers.

Work with the business Trial Balance as a lead sheet, ensuring you can see the prior year's figures. All balance sheet items should have a work paper supporting the reconciled figure. For example:

1. Cash at bank needs a bank reconciliation plus bank statement showing the date as at 30th June.
2. MV chattel mortgage, should have a reconciliation of payments and term charges expensed, and closing statement and preferably a copy of the loan document.
3. Director's loan account should at least have a transaction listing report printed. They are either lending money to the company or taking money from the company. This should be accounted for accurately.
4. ATO accounts reconcile to lodgements, or cash versus accrual reconciliation.
5. Income Tax reconciliation work paper balances the financial statements to the tax return.
6. Provision for income tax work paper, reconciles the tax instalments paid to the ATO, together with past and future tax obligations.

7. Carried forward losses schedule, if required, should be maintained and can be used for tax planning purposes.
8. Franking account workpapers should be updated annually.
9. Income accounts should have a summary reconciliation to lodged BAS with any cash/accrual adjustment add backs.
10. Payroll: wages and superannuation expense should always have a work paper reconciled to lodged STP report/ reported BAS.
11. Repairs & maintenance expense accounts are often audited, ensure you have a detailed transaction listing printed off. Maybe new equipment needs to be purchased if maintenance costs are too high?
12. COGS can be checked to the ATO industry benchmark. Are purchases in line with sales? Do you suspect any cash dealings not reported? Has the client left themselves open for an ATO audit?

https://www.ato.gov.au/businesses-and-organisations/income-deductions-and-concessions/small-business-benchmarks/benchmarks-by-industry

Any expenses that have increased substantially compared to the previous year, should have a work paper file note with an investigation as to why there is movement. It might be materials, wages, super and sub-contracting fees all increased by 33%, correlating to an increase of sales by 75%. If the profits are down for a business, then investigate why they are down and make a file note.

Your investigations should lead to discussions with your client. Tax planning opportunities exist everywhere. A good network of referring professionals will assist you to make the relevant suggestions. Any tax planning suggestions must be in writing with the supporting documentation you used to make those recommendations. It is useful to build loyalty with your client if they feel that you are solving their tax problems.

You should keep what is referred to as a *permanent file* for each client. This file contains all contracts and equipment invoices, doc IDs, business structure flow diagram and Div 7a loan agreements. Keep in mind that you are not permitted to file documents that you used to identify your client such as a driver's license or passport. You are required to identify your client with a 100-point ID check but you are not allowed to keep a copy of the documents you used to do it, simply make a note in the Permanent File that you have done it and what used to get a positive ID.

Keep a log of any management issues you've discussed with your client. Your client will appreciate your interest in their business and will be a lot less inclined to dump you as their accountant if they feel you have built up a substantial knowledge of how that business operates. Always keep in mind though that your client knows more about running their business than you do so don't tell them how to work, just how to organise.

CHAPTER NINE

Australian Securities and Investments Commission ASIC

The role ASIC plays under the act is to maintain, facilitate and improve the performance of the financial system and entities in it, promote confident and informed participation by investors and consumers in the financial system and administer the law effectively and with minimal procedural requirements.

It is important that a Tax Agent in public practice can assist their clients with their ASIC obligations. Your corporate clients will expect you to be able to provide this service. The overall term for this is called looking after your corporate client's *company secretarial administration.* This includes setting up a company, ensuring that the corporate records are accurate and align with you client's design for the company structure, assisting in changes to the ASIC register as required by the client and managing the annual reporting obligations for each of your corporate clients.

It is appropriate to charge a fee for such services. Usually that fee takes two forms, the first is an annual fee for managing the recuring corporate reporting requirements and secondly, fee for service if the client asks you to amend the ASIC record or set up a company.

To perform those tasks, you will need to become an ASIC Agent. To obtain a registration you will need to be managing ten or more corporate clients.

It is highly recommended that one of the first things that you do when you acquire a corporate client is to put them on your ASIC Register and extract a listing of the corporate record held by ASIC for that client and ensure that your client confirms, in writing—everything should always be in writing—that the ASIC record is correct. You would be surprised by the frequency of misalignments between what your client believes is on the ASIC record and what actual is on the ASIC record. Common areas of divergence include: the company has changed its registered address, directors have changed, the share structure has changed, and in all such instances the ASIC record may not have been updated. An incorrect company record can lead to serious consequences for retiring directors, the issuance of legal documents to the company and penalties for not providing a timely update to the ASIC records.

All directors are required to have a government issued director's ID. A director's ID is a unique identifier a director applies for once and keeps forever. It helps prevent the use of false or fraudulent director identities. You do not need a director ID for each company, each director must have their own ID. All directors of a company, registered Australian body, registered foreign company or Aboriginal and Torres Strait Islander corporation need a director's ID. ASIC is responsible for enforcing director's ID and offences are set out in the *Corporations Act 2001*. It's a criminal offence if directors do not apply on time to obtain an ID and penalties may apply.

A director is responsible for overseeing the affairs of the company. They must comply with all legal obligations as a director under the *Corporations Act 2001*. This is the case even if an agent or manager is appointed to look after the company's affairs. The director needs to be fully up to date on what their company is doing, including its financial position.

As the Tax Agent you need to be up to date with changes in the corporations law to ensure that you guide you clients appropriately. When a director makes a business decision as a company director, they must, among other things, ensure that they:

- make the decision in good faith and for a proper purpose;
- do not have a material personal interest in the decision and make it in the best interests of the company;
- find out and assess how any decision will affect the company's business performance, especially if it involves a significant amount of the company's money or could have a material impact on the company's reputation or asset values;
- keep informed about the company's financial position and performance, most notably ensuring the company can pay its debts on time;
- get trusted professional advice when assistance is needed to make an informed decision; and
- lodge and pay its taxes on time and always make full and frank disclosure to the ATO.

There are penalties and consequences, including civil penalties, compensation proceedings and criminal charges, for directors who fail to comply with their obligations under Australian law.

As a company director it is important that they understand:

- the company owns the assets and the money in the company's bank accounts, so they cannot treat company property, assets or funds as if they are their own;

- the company is responsible for paying debts incurred by the company, which may include trade creditors, employees and statutory bodies such as the Australian Taxation Office and ASIC;

- if there are reasonable grounds to suspect that the company is in financial difficulty, a director should consider obtaining appropriate professional advice regarding insolvency;

- any money invested in the company (e.g. through loans to the company or by owners or investors buying shares in the company) belongs to the company and must be used for a proper company purpose;

- the owners or members (shareholders) of the company are entitled to take a dividend payment from the company but only after the company has ensured it has the ability to pay its debts owing to trade creditors and other types of creditors who have lent money to the company, employees and statutory authorities;

- while a company is usually responsible for paying its debts, a director may under certain circumstances and in relation to specific debts become personally liable for a company's liabilities. This generally occurs when a director breaches their legal obligations (e.g. the company continues to trade while it is insolvent) or when members or directors have provided personal guarantees when borrowing money;

- also, it is important to note, certain employee-related debts such as PAYG withheld or superannuation will become the personal liability of the director should the company be liquidated without having sufficient funds to cover such debts; and
- if the company fails to meet a PAYG withholding or SGC liability or lodge returns by the due date, the director may become personally liable for any penalty.

It is extremely useful for the public practicing Tax Agent to obtain an ASIC agent's license. There are no specific requirements to obtain such a license other than good standing but you must be looking after ten or more corporate clients. With an ASIC agent's number you can log directly into the ASIC register and perform tasks such as listing the company's organisational details, change director or shareholder details and other associated details such as registered address. When making such changes or obtaining such information you will require the client's written consent or have them sign the relevant form before you lodge it. You can also review where a company stands regarding any outstanding ASIC debts.

If you have an ASIC agent's number and put the corporate client onto your agent register then you will receive important statements from ASIC regarding your client. Some clients will not want you to do this preferring instead to look after such matters themselves, so it is important to get their consent and agree to your fees for such services. You should encourage your client to let you do it. The benefit in you doing it is not just the fees, but you can ensure that you get any alerts your client receives regarding their obligations as required by ASIC. The most pertinent of these notifications is the annual ASIC statement which brings with it an invoice for the annual registration fees for the company. If those ASIC fees are unpaid it could lead to the deregistration of the company. Like all such administrative issues, if something goes wrong it will be your fault. So, it is important to have on file your reminders to the clients to pay such fees. If the ASIC statements are coming to you, along with any other ASIC notification to your client, then you will know that you need to chase your clients to meet those obligations.

Tax Agent Pathway can assist you with all company secretarial requirements whilst you are building your database of clients.

You need to establish an account with a reputable firm that creates companies and trusts, such firms usually are owned by lawyers. Those firms can assist you in the creation of companies and trusts. You can of course do it yourself through the ASIC agent login but for the minimal premium such firms charge for the service, over and above the ASIC fees, it's hardly worth your time.

Please also refer to the upcoming chapter of all issues related to servicing your company clients.

CHAPTER TEN

Company Clients

I start with company clients because they, and other clients conducting a business, should be the heart of your practice. You can't build a practice on personal tax returns (ITRs) because they are low sales value per unit, usually transient, and the ATO is trying to get people to do their ITR directly with them and in pursuit of that objective they are changing the tax law to simplify ITR lodgement. Clients pay better for company and business returns because they are harder to get right and those clients are looking to obtain the best tax result. You can also obtain other fees from helping them comply with the now myriads of administrative requirements piled on small business by successive government agencies.

To begin with create an onboarding list of questions for your business clients. That list should at a minimum include the following (TAP can assist you with this list):

- the names, addresses and TFNs of all shareholders;
- the names, addresses and TFNs of all directors and their director's ID. If they don't have a director's ID insist that they obtain one and advise you;

- registered address of the business;
- a short description of what the business does;
- a comprehensive signed engagement letter; and,
- a record of you obtaining a 100 point ID of each member, but do not keep the source documents for that identification on file.

Also ensure that you:

- do your ethical letter to the previous accountant;
- put them on your tax portal and on your ASIC agent's register;
- do the ATO client agent linking which is required for all entities except individual clients (but there is talk of that being brought in for individuals as well); and

Always have a meeting with your client before you prepare the tax return. Talk to them about their business over the past year and changes that have occurred relevant to their tax position. It is best to have an ATO pre-fill listing in front of you to aid in that discussion as well as a copy of last year's return. Keep notes of the discussion and put them on file each year. There are systems available that record your meeting and turns that recording into hardcopy copy for you to file and to send to your client.

Obtain an ASIC listing for the company once you have them on your ASIC register (TAP can assist you with this) and review it with your client to ensure that the shareholding and directorships and all other details are as per your client's expectations. Include in this review a discussion of any outstanding ASIC fees.

When sending the ethical letter to the previous accountant (standard drafts are available from TAP) confirm to them that you have been asked to take over the account and, attempt to get the reason for them parting ways with your new client. You can ask for the relevant paperwork held by the accountant belonging to the client including the company register. The accountant is legally obliged to hand over all paperwork except for their own work product. They are not obliged to tell you why the client is leaving.

Upload all papers to your standard file—see chapter on working papers.

When entering the client onto your ATO Tax portal, review the status of the client in regard to any outstanding lodgement obligations and any outstanding tax debts. You need to obtain a commitment from your client to bring all outstanding lodgements up to date and to make appropriate arrangements regarding any unpaid tax and superannuation liabilities.

Your important initial considerations should also include:

- advising the client of the benefits of having the appropriate ledger software if the client is using manual administration. We recommend that the client obtains and pays for the ledger software subscription themselves so that they retain ownership of the data;
- Include an explanation of the benefits of setting up bank feeds directly to that software;
- review the client's stance on amending prior year returns should you identified errors made by the previous accountant;
- include in the discussion of any outstanding obligations the client may have with the ATO what the client's intentions are regarding making them compliant. If the

client is not prepared to bring their ATO obligations up to date or to pay any outstanding tax debts, or make arrangements for outstanding tax debts with the ATO, then do not accept them as a client;

- ensure that the franking account has been reconciled with tax lodgements and is up to date;
- ensure that all ledger reconciliations are up to date;
- discuss personal drawings from the company accounts and the tax implications for the client personally and the need to set up a loan agreement, Div 7a Agreements, should the client have taken a loan from the company; and,
- discuss Workcover and appropriate general insurances.

Here is an example of the checklist you should develop to assist you prepare the returns. This list will no doubt have to be updated on a regular basis to keep up with changes on the act.

2024 Company Tax Return Checklist

ITEM	Yes	No	N/A
• Is the company a small business entity (SBE) (i.e., a business that meets the $10 million aggregated turnover threshold)? If so, confirm which concessions the company is entitled to.			
• If the company is an SBE, is it using the simplified depreciation rules?			
• If the company is not an SBE, does it meet the $50 million aggregated turnover threshold? If so, confirm which concessions the company is entitled to.			
• Is the company a base rate entity in 2024?			
• If the company was not incorporated in Australia, has the company's residency been determined in line with Taxation Ruling TR 2018/5?			

• Is the company required to lodge a Reportable Tax Position schedule?			
Income			
• Check for any cash earnings or payments that may not have been accounted for.			
• Ensure trading stock figure equals closing stock account on the profit and loss account.			
• Agree investment income e.g., dividends, interest with external source data.			
• Have employee contributions for FBT purposes been taken up in the accounts and appropriate GST journal entries made?			
• Has the company made/received an allocation of profits from a professional firm? If yes, consider ATO former guidance 'Assessing the risk: allocation of profits within professional firms' (see Practical Compliance Guideline PCG 2021/4 which applies from 1 July 2022).			
Expenses			
• Put through depreciation entries and agree asset balances to depreciation schedule (including journaling asset purchases and sales).			
• For asset purchases has the company determined its policy on depreciating additions (on prime cost or diminishing value) where eligible (and assets cannot be immediately written off under the SBE regime).			
• Perform annual entries for lease and hire purchase transactions.			
• Look for unusual balances of the profit and loss items (perhaps compare balances with the prior year).			
• Accounting fees—check against billings.			
• If fees are being paid to a service entity, ensure that the service fees are in line with Taxation Ruling TR 2006/2.			
• When prepayments were made during the year that cover services in the following tax year, has deductibility been determined in accordance with the prepayment rules? (Note that from 1 July 2020, businesses with aggregated turnover less than $50 million can immediately deduct			

certain prepaid expenditure where the payment covers a period of 12 months or less that ends in the next income year.)		
• Where any part of a prepayment was non-deductible in 2023 as a result of the prepayment rules, is the amount deductible in 2024?		
• Has non-deductible entertainment expenditure been added back for tax purposes unless it was included in the company's FBT return?		
• Have other non-deductible expenses been added back for tax purposes?		
• Have movements in provisions been adjusted for (e.g., provisions for annual leave and long service leave)?		
• Has the company paid the required superannuation guarantee contributions for employees? If not, ensure that a superannuation guarantee charge statement has been lodged with the ATO.		
• Were employee superannuation contributions 'made' in the current income year per Taxation Ruling TR 2010/1 (to determine deductibility)?		
• Do wages on the income statements reconcile to the general ledger and lodged business activity statements?		
• Has the payment summary information been lodged with the ATO (where required)?		
• For single touch payroll purposes, has a finalisation declaration been performed for each employee?		
• Did the company fail to meet its PAYGW obligations to withhold or notify the Commissioner? If so, a deduction is denied unless the taxpayer voluntarily discloses the issue to the ATO.		
• If the company is liable for workers compensation, have all payments been made in relevant year?		
• If the company is not registered for payroll tax, should it be?		
• Has the June 2024 FBT instalment been deducted per Taxation Ruling TR 95/24?		

• If the company is engaging contractors, have you checked whether they would be classified as employees for the purposes of PAYG withholding, superannuation guarantee, workers compensation, payroll tax, etc.?			
• Have you considered whether the company may be eligible for the R&D tax incentive or the digital tax offset?			
• Ensure that the financials are in line with ATO benchmarks and investigate discrepancies where necessary.			
• If there are prior year losses, consider whether the company loss recoupment rules are met.			
Balance sheet			
• Agree bank and loan balances against statements/bank reconciliations.			
• Agree hire purchase balances against schedule.			
• Agree debtor and creditor balances.			
• Verify with client all plant and equipment are still on hand (i.e., identify sales, purchases, items scrapped).			
• Agree trading stock figures to stock take.			
• Verify all other balance sheet balances.			
• Do the debt and equity rules apply in respect of shareholders' loans? (only relevant where turnover exceeds $20 million).			
• Have the Division 7A provisions been considered in respect of loans, payments and debts forgiven to shareholders and their associates?			
• Have the Division 7A provisions been considered in respect of unpaid distributions from trusts?			
PSI			
• If the company derived any personal services income (PSI), is the company carrying on a personal services business (PSB)?			
• If not, consider the PSI that must be attributed to an individual.			

• If yes, consider whether the Commissioner could apply Part IVA to the arrangement.			
Capital gains			
• Has the company sold, redeemed, or disposed of an asset in any other way during the year, have exemptions, reductions, or rollovers been considered?			
• For any share issues or transfers made during the year, have the value shifting rules been considered?			
• If the company holds any pre-CGT assets (acquired prior to 20 September 1985), have there been any significant changes to the shareholding of the company since 20 September 1985?			
GST			
• If the company is not registered for GST, should it be registered?			
• If the company is registered for GST, do the GST accounts reconcile to the BAS lodged?			
• Does the income declared in the activity statements reconcile with the income disclosed in the tax return?			
International			
• Does the company have transactions/loans with international related parties? If yes, consider the transfer pricing rules, and consider whether an international dealings schedule has been completed (at the time of writing, the 2024 form was yet to be released—but the 2023 form can be downloaded at https://www.ato.gov.au/forms-andinstructions/international-dealings-schedule-2023).			
• Does the company have a bank account in another country or buy/sell products offshore? If so, consider the foreign exchange rules.			
Dividends and franking			
• Has a distribution statement been prepared and provided to shareholder/s and a minute prepared?			
• Is there documentation prepared by the directors that demonstrates that the requirements of s 254T of the *Corporations Act 2001* have been satisfied? See Taxation Ruling TR 2012/5.			

• Have the benchmark franking rules been satisfied?			
• Has the franking account been prepared?			
• Is there a franking account deficit at years end?			
• Has the company's corporate rate for imputation purposes been determined?			

An important consideration when doing company returns is the possible need to do a FBT Return. FBT, Fringe Benefit Tax, is a tax that employers pay on the costs associated with non-monetary benefits paid to an employee or their associate, such as a family. FBT is calculated on the taxable value of the benefits provided. This is separate to income tax. The tax is levied based on a FBT return submitted by the client.

The FBT tax can be avoided if the recipient reimburses the business for the costs incurred in providing the benefit, but with company clients the entity will still have to summit a return even if it is nil.

FBT Covers the following most common benefits provided:

1. Employee credit card payments.
2. Car loan payments for a car owned by the employee.
3. Car parking—pre-tax-contribution.
4. Salary packaging.
5. Driving business vehicles.
6. Entertainment.

FBT is a specialised topic and covers employer obligations, employee contribution and record keeping. If you are not familiar with this, please avail yourself of the training provided by TAP.

ATO wants company taxpayers to register for FBT return even if reimbursement payments are made to make it a nil return.

For non-corporate clients you will have to lodge a *return not necessary*.

An amendment to an FBT return can generally only be made within three years from the date the FBT return being lodged. Where tax has been avoided, the amendment can be made within six years of lodgement. In cases of fraud or evasion, there is no time limit on when the ATO can amend an assessment.

CHAPTER ELEVEN

Personal Tax Clients

There is no future in the tax services industry for providers who are cheap. Charge enough for an ITR to ensure that you can provide a quality and thorough service. Clients who demand cheap prices are often the most demanding of your time and are almost always transient. They will shop your services next year looking for a cheaper price and you will go backwards trying to build your client base.

Do not accept a client who is pressuring you for a refund regardless of the actual figures. You cannot assert to your client when promoting your services that you can guarantee a tax refund or that you will obtain a bigger tax refund that any other provider.

Taxpayers looking to mislead the ATO to obtain a tax refund will get caught and you will have a lot of explaining to do. Always live up to the ethical standards required of a Tax Agent.

Once you have selected a client, you need to identify them. The ATO has specific requirements regarding the identification of the taxpayer. You are not permitted to keep on file copies of personal identifiers such as a driver's license or passport once you have sighted them for identification purposes.

Set conditions with your client, in writing, on the provision of your services. You do this usually by providing the client with an engagement letter. With personal tax return clients, ITRs, if they are not associated with a business in your practice then an engagement letter is not necessary. Their signature on the tax return is sufficient to authorise you to act on their behalf with the ATO.

Add the client to your tax portal and then check on the portal for any outstanding debts and whether they are up to date with their lodgements. Do not act for a client who refuses to make suitable arrangements regarding outstanding ATO obligations. You may offer them your service for a fee to bring their lodgements up to date or negotiate a payment plan with the ATO for any outstanding debts. Keep and file all appropriate working papers.

Ensure that you get part or all of your service fee up front and come to a clear understanding, in writing, in regard to the payment of any part of your fee that is not paid up front.

When you are doing the return and your client has a spouse it is advisable to do both partners together or at least obtain a copy of the partners return if one has already been lodged. This is particularly relevant where there are shared income producing assets such as a rental property. You do not want to be claiming expenses twice and you want to be clear about income splitting. If they do own a property together then the income split should be in line with the ownership rights.

A few basic considerations:

- access and review last year's return and look for year-on-year changes;
- ensure that you sight all major receipts. You are not required to audit but you are required to be diligent in your preparation of the return;
- ensure the client has logbooks for milage claims for each vehicle used that contain at least 12 consecutive weeks of vehicle use;
- record support for working from home claims;
- obtain and review the prefills from the tax portal. The prefill may also report other information such as disposal of assets, dividends, interest, and taxable payments received under an ABN and warnings about higher-than-expected tax deductions in a prior year; and,
- ensure you keep a record of the client's signed return. Electronic signatures are acceptable. The client signing the return means that they accept responsibility for the information provided in the return. Whilst the Tax Agent is not an auditor of that information, the agent is required by the ATO to be diligent in the collection and lodgement of that information.

Here is an example of the checklist you should develop to assist you prepare the returns. This list will no doubt have to be updated on a regular basis to keep up with changes on the act.

2024 Individual Tax Return Checklist

	Yes	No	N/A
• Download and review ATO pre-filling report.			
• Did the client's residency status change during the year? If so, consider a part-year tax-free threshold.			
• Has CGT event I1 been triggered?			
• Was taxpayer in Australia on a working holiday visa 417 or 462?			
• Employment income and deductions.			
• Salary and wages.			
• Allowances, earnings, tips and directors' fees.			
• Reportable fringe benefits.			
• Reportable employer superannuation contributions.			
• Lump sum payments A and B.			
• Lump sum payment D (not subject to tax and no disclosure is required in the return).			
• Lump sum E—lump sum payments in arrears.			
• Employment termination payments.			
• Shares or rights under an Employee Share Scheme.			
Deductions			
• Car used for work purposes (and not reimbursed)— consider log book or cents per km method.			
• Travel expenses for work (where a travel allowance was received, consider the substantiation exception—refer TR 2004/6).			
• Expenses for clothing, uniform, laundry, or protective gear (e.g., sunglasses, sunscreen, compulsory uniform)?			
• Self-education expenses (e.g., course fees, materials, travel, parking, stationery, books, depreciation of equipment, etc).			
• Consider if fully allowable given tightened rules under TR 2024/3.			

• Other expenses (union fees, overtime meals, telephone, internet, books, journals, subscriptions, workshops and home office expenses which must be claimed in accordance with PCG 2023/1 where no details of actual costs).			
Government payments			
• Government allowances and payments (e.g., Jobseeker payment, youth allowance, Austudy, parenting payment [partnered], sickness allowance, etc).			
• Government pensions and allowances (e.g., age pension, carer payment, parenting payment [single], age service pension, etc).			
• Consider eligibility for Senior and pensioners tax offset (SAPTO)?			
Superannuation benefits and annuities			
• Superannuation income streams or annuities.			
• Superannuation lump sum.			
• Consider whether a SAPTO or income stream tax offset is available.			
• Foreign pension or annuity.			
• For assessable foreign pension or annuity, consider a deduction for the un-deducted purchase price.			
Investment amounts			
• Interest on bank accounts, term deposits or received from the ATO and any associated TFN tax.			
• Dividends on shares.			
• Franking credits attached to dividends—consider: ✦ has the 45-day holding period rule been satisfied? or ✦ is the small shareholder exemption satisfied (no more than $5,000 imputation credits from all sources received in the year)?			
• Tax offset for exploration credits received or is individual the principal of special disability trust?			
• Managed fund distributions.			
• Rental property income and expenses.			
• Interest, fees, borrowing costs, management costs related to earning interest income.			

• Interest, fees, borrowing costs, management costs, journals/subscriptions related to earning dividend income.			
• For contribution to an early-stage venture capital limited partnership (ESVCLP), consider eligibility for tax offset.			
• Consider 20% offset for investor in an early-stage innovation company (subject to a $10,000 or $200,000 cap depending on nature of investor).			
• Trust beneficiaries and partners.			
• Distributions from trust or partnership.			
• Distribution from a trust, company or partnership on which family trust distribution tax has been paid—not assessable but must be disclosed to calculate income for Medicare levy surcharge purposes.			
• Where partnership loss was incurred, consider the non-commercial loss provisions.			
• Consider cost base adjustments for non-assessable payments from a unit trust.			
• For beneficiary/partner of SBE, consider small business tax offset that applies to unincorporated businesses.			
Business amounts			
• Carrying on a business as a sole trader.			
• Sole traders subject to the PSI rules.			
• Where there are business losses or brought forward non-commercial losses, consider non-commercial loss rules.			
• Deductible farm management deposits and assessable withdrawals.			
• Consider the small business tax offset that applies to unincorporated businesses.			
Personal services income (PSI) amounts			
• Attributed PSI from a personal services entity (PSE).			
• Deductible net PSI loss from a PSE.			
Capital gains or losses			
• Capital gain or loss on disposal or non-arm's length transfer of capital assets (real estate, shares, managed fund withdrawals, etc).			

• Foreign resident CGT withholding amount withheld.			
• Capital losses carried forward from 2023.			
Other income amounts			
• Foreign investors or individuals receiving foreign income.			
• Bonus from a life insurance policy or a friendly society.			
• Forestry managed investment scheme income.			
• Income earned from sharing economy (if not rent or business).			
• Assessable amount released under First Home Super Saver scheme.			
• Amounts released by super fund that exceed liability on a release authority.			
• Taxable scholarships.			
• Royalties.			
• Assessable balancing adjustment from disposal/loss or destruction of depreciating asset.			
• Professional income as an author, musician, artist, or sportsperson.			
• Reimbursement of tax-related expenses.			
• Bonus amounts on friendly society bonds.			
Other deductions			
• Low value pool deductions.			
• Gifts or donations to deductible gift recipient, registered political party, or independent member of Parliament (consider spreading over 5 years where beneficial).			
• Costs of managing tax affairs (e.g., Tax Agent's fees, travel costs to obtain advice, quantity surveyors report, ATO interest paid, etc)—divide into: ✦ interest charged by the ATO; ✦ litigation costs; and ✦ other expenses incurred in managing tax affairs.			
• Deductible personal superannuation contributions (ensure a notice of intent to claim or vary a deduction for personal contributions form has been provided to the fund, and the taxpayer has received an acknowledgement from the fund).			

• Consider the making of catch-up concessional contributions (if eligible).			
• Capital expenditure directly connected to a project.			
• Deductible payments to a forestry managed investment scheme.			
• Election expenses for local, territory, state and federal candidates.			
• Income protection, sickness or accident insurance premiums.			
• Expenses incurred in deriving income from the sharing economy returned as income at Item 24.			
• Five-year write off for certain business-related capital expenses not claimed in full before business ceased under blackhole provisions of section 40-880 of the ITAA 1997.			
• Immediate deduction for certain start-up expenses relating to proposed business structure under section 40-880.			
• Self-education expenses incurred in doing course of study to satisfy requirements of taxable scholarship.			
Other tax offsets			
• Maintenance of a relative (including invalid spouse, carer spouse, invalid relative [child, brother or sister 16 years old or older], spouse's invalid relative, parent, or spouse's parent).			
• Landcare or water facility tax offset brought forward from an earlier year.			
• Contributions to a complying superannuation fund on behalf of a spouse.			
• Zone offset for individuals living in remote area of Australia or working overseas with Australian Defence Force or as prescribed member of United Nations armed force.			
Other items			
• Revenue losses brought forward from prior years—separately disclosing losses from primary production and/or non-primary production business.			

• Consider excepted income of minors.			
• Complete adjusted taxable income labels.			
• Complete spouse items.			
• Complete private health insurance details where relevant.			
• Is the client eligible for a Medicare levy reduction or exemption taking into account increased thresholds for the 2023-24 year?			
• Super co-contribution for eligible personal superannuation contributions (only relevant where taxpayer was under 71 on 30 June 2024 with total income is less than $58,445).			
Tax estimate			
• Consider outstanding HELP, TSL or SFSS debts (with regard to HELP debt repayment thresholds for the year ended 30 June 2024).			

CHAPTER TWELVE

Trusts

A trust is an obligation for a person or other entity to hold property or assets for and on behalf of beneficiaries. A trust is a fiduciary relationship, a contract in the form of a deed, not a legal entity.

If your client wants to set up a trust, they need to keep in mind that trust structures:

- can be expensive to set-up and operate;
- require a formal trust deed that outlines how the trust operates. The deed needs to be prepared by a licensed provider;
- require the trustee to undertake formal yearly administrative tasks;
- the trustee needs to ensure that the assets are protected; and,
- trusts can be difficult to dissolve or make changes to once established.

Do not try and draft the deed yourself, potentially working off some template you found online. You're not licensed to do that work. Brief a licensed provider and get them to draft it. Search trust deed providers.

If your client operates their business as a trust, the trustee is legally responsible for its operations. That means the trustee is liable for the debts or other liabilities of the trust. For that reason, it is recommended that the trustee of a trust be a company, providing some asset protection.

There are several different types of trusts, the most common being a *discretionary trust,* often called a *family trust,* due to their high flexibility in regard to disbursements from the trust. The trustee of a family trust has the choice to determine how income and capital earned by the trust is distributed among beneficiaries. That distribution determination can be changed from year to year making that form of trust ideal for tax planning. The benefit to tax planning using a family trust is that the earnings from the assets within the trust can be distributed after considering the income of each beneficiary prior to receiving that distribution thus ensuring that each beneficiary is in the lowest possible tax bracket each year. So, these trusts are primarily used by families for tax planning and asset management offering significant tax benefits provided that the complex tax rules governing trusts are carefully followed. Failure to manage the trust correctly can result in unexpected tax outcomes. When preparing the trust tax return, pay particular attention to the establishment of the distribution minutes. The minutes need to follow the law and the rules in the trust deed and they need to be made chronologically within the applicable tax year. You need to keep a copy of the minutes authorising the distributions from the trust on file.

If you are doing the tax return for any type of trust, or the returns for those receiving a distribution from a trust, you need to review the trust deed and the applicable minutes.

Fixed trusts are where the beneficiaries have fixed entitlements to the trust's income and capital as specified in the trust deed. This structure is ideal for situations where clear and predetermined asset distribution is required, such as business partnerships or joint investments or the ownership of real assets. A common example of a fixed trust is a basic will or estate, where assets are distributed according to fixed instructions outlined in the trust deed.

Unit trusts operate similarly to fixed trusts, with beneficiaries holding units that represent their share of the trust's assets. This structure is popular for joint ventures and investment proposals, as units can be transferred or sold, offering greater flexibility in ownership. However, unlike discretionary trusts, unit trusts do not provide flexibility in distributions. They do, however, allow multiple families to enjoy some benefits of the trust structure without the family group restrictions typically associated with discretionary trusts.

In discretionary trusts, a "family group restriction" occurs when the beneficiaries are limited to eligible family members, as defined by the Australian Taxation Office (ATO), for the purpose of claiming certain tax concessions. This restriction is achieved through a "family trust election" (FTE), where the trustee limits the beneficiaries to the defined family group. An FTE can only be made if the trust passes the family control test at the end of the specified income year, meaning that only the individual specified in the relevant FTE or members of their family or their advisers are in control of the trust. An FTE can't be made for a trust that has previously had an FTE revoked.

Hybrid trusts combine features of discretionary and fixed trusts. They offer flexibility in distributing income at the trustee's discretion while maintaining fixed entitlements for capital. This makes them suitable for families or groups pooling resources for business projects. Hybrid trusts are generally only seen in widely held, large-scale and often listed arrangements.

Testamentary trusts are established through a will and take effect upon the death of the trustor. These trusts are designed to protect assets and provide for dependants, often with specific instructions on how and when the assets should be distributed.

Charitable trusts are created to fund philanthropic causes. These trusts are tax-effective and must follow strict regulations to ensure funds are used for their intended charitable purposes. They're ideal for individuals or organisations looking to make a lasting social impact.

Special Disability Trusts are designed to support the care and accommodation the needs of family members with severe disabilities. They provide financial security for the beneficiary while allowing contributors to benefit from social security concessions. While these trusts sound useful, often the reality is they are not as useful or as tax effective as perhaps the intent was when they were original designed.

Superannuation funds operate under a trust structure. These funds manage retirement savings, offering tax advantages and ensuring financial security in retirement. Self-Managed Superannuation Funds (SMSFs) provide individuals with greater control over their investments (see the Chapter on SMSFs).

Finally, *Bare trusts* are simple structures where the trustee holds assets on behalf of a beneficiary who has full control over them. These trusts are often used for temporary purposes, such as holding property for minors until they reach legal age.

Selecting the right trust depends on the client's goals and circumstances. You need to consider the following issues:

- what does the client want to achieve? (e.g., asset protection, tax planning, estate management);
- who will benefit from the trust? (e.g., family, business partners, charitable organisations);
- how much flexibility do they need? (e.g., fixed entitlements vs. discretionary distributions);
- what are the legal and tax implications?
- choosing the wrong type of trust can be a serious mistake. Misaligned structures can limit flexibility or expose assets to risks. Consideration of the types of activities and assets the trust will be involved in is very important. The wrong trust structure may lock in inflexibilities and cash flow issues for your client;
- using a trust comes with strict legal and tax obligations. Failing to meet these can result in penalties. These can be significant and the ATO's power of review can be unlimited in some circumstances;
- trusts must distribute their taxable income every year and this can pose problems with the accumulation of working capital as the beneficiaries, or the trustee must pay tax on funds they may not receive immediately if funds are retained; and
- losses cannot be distributed out of a trust.

A trustee technically has ownership of any assets held in the trust, because the trust itself is not a legal entity but the trustee does not derive any benefit from that ownership. The trustee may become liable for any damages arising from non-compliance with the trust deed, and for this reason it is advisable to insert a company as trustee. If the trustee will be liable for tax payable on undistributed earnings. Generally, the income earned by the trust is taxed in the hands of the beneficiary.

Whilst a trust is not a separate legal entity it must have a TFN and an ABN and is required to lodge a tax return, Form T, irrespective of whether it distributes 100% of its income to the beneficiaries. That tax return must include a statement of distribution specifying what each beneficiary received from the trust. Income accumulated by the trust forms part of the capital (corpus) of the trust and the income tax on the rates applicable to the trustee. Be aware of the tax rates applicable to deceased estates.

Here are some of the things you need to look at when reviewing trust distributions for the trust tax return. These considerations need to be reviewed in light of any changes in the tax law:

- were distributions correctly allocated to income and capital beneficiaries by 30 June, or an earlier date if required by the trust deed?
- has a determination of income been made where required and if the deed permits?
- if the trustee has attempted to stream franked dividends or capital gains for tax purposes, was a written record made by the relevant dates to make beneficiaries specifically entitled?
- is the trust in a positive income position—both trust (distributable) income and net (taxable) income so that franking credits can pass through to the beneficiaries?
- will beneficiaries of a discretionary trust be entitled to claim franking credits attached to distributions based on: the small shareholder exemption; or the trustee having a family trust election in place?

- have the Division 7A provisions been considered in respect of unpaid distributions to companies? See TD 2022/11 which applies from 1 July 2022;
- does someone other than the presently entitled beneficiary actually benefit from the trust income (e.g., trustee gives, or lends the funds to another party)? If so, does section 100A of the ITAA 1936 apply having regard to TR 2022/4 and PCG 2022/2;
- if the trustee appointed income to tax exempt entities, was full payment made or a written statement provided to the entity by 31 August 2023? (refer s 100AA ITAA 1936); and, does the taxable portion of the distribution breach the 'benchmark percentage' set out in the anti-avoidance rules? (s 100AB ITAA 1936);
- are beneficiaries presently entitled to all income of the trust (i.e., determine whether the trustee is liable for tax on any portion of the income)?
- if trust (distributable) income is different to taxable income, has the taxable income allocated to each beneficiary been calculated using the proportionate method (adjusted for streamed franked dividends and capital gains)?
- has the proportionate method been applied in accordance with the Commissioner's guidelines in TR 2012/D1 (particularly relevant where trust income includes franking credits)?
- is the trustee required to pay tax on behalf of any beneficiaries (e.g., non-residents, minors)? Warning: a discretionary trust distribution to a non-resident beneficiary comprising capital gains on non-taxable Australian property (e.g., listed shares) is assessed to the trustee under s 98(3) ITAA 1936. See *Peter Greensill*

Family Co Pty Ltd (trustee) v FCT [2020] FCA 559 and TD 2019/D6;

- where the trust has a family trust election in place, has any distribution been made to entities outside of the family group?
- did the trustee obtain TFNs from all beneficiaries (excluding minors, non-residents and tax-exempt entities) prior to appointing income to the end of the income year?
- has the trust complied with the TFN reporting obligations for closely held trusts? and
- if the trust has distributed to another trust, have the trustee beneficiary reporting rules been complied with (only necessary where there is no family trust election in place)?

Trusts are subject to complex measures which need to be satisfied before deducting losses from prior income years. There are different tests that need to be passed depending on whether the trust is a fixed trust or a non-fixed trust or excepted trusts.

If your client operates their business as a trust and they incur a tax loss, they can't distribute the loss to the trust's beneficiaries. Losses must be quarantined in a trust to be carried forward by the trust indefinitely until they can be offset against future net income. It is possible to use those losses as deductions against income in the trust in future income years if the trust satisfies certain tests relating to ownership or control of the trust. If the trust terminates before the losses can be offset against income, they are lost.

The trust loss legislation is contained in Schedule 2F to the Income Tax Assessment Act 1936. How to claim a tax loss on your trust tax return is explained (currently) in question 27 of the trust tax return instructions. To claim a tax loss on your trust tax, return a trust must have made a family trust election or interposed entity election.

As a side note, although a trustee often undertakes the day-to-day management of a trust, effective control of a trust generally rests with the person/s who can dismiss or appoint a trustee or change the trust deed, usually called the *appointer*.

A Family Trust Election (FTE) and Interposed Entity Election (IEE) must be completed if the trustee:

- has made or is making a family trust election;
- is revoking or varying an existing family trust election;
- has made or is making an interposed entity election;
- is revoking an existing interposed entity election;
- an FTE must specify a person as the individual whose family group is to be taken into account in relation to the election (referred to as the specified individual, primary individual or test individual throughout Schedule 2F);
- the specified individual has no additional rights or responsibilities and doesn't even need to be directly associated with the trust;
- only one individual can be specified in an FTE;
- where an FTE is being made in respect of an earlier year of income, the specified individual's date of birth must be on or before the beginning of the income year specified for the commencement of the FTE;
- the specified individual must also be alive at the time the election is made; and
- the FTE isn't affected by the death of the individual specified in the FTE—the members of the family group are still determined by reference to that individual.

A consequence of a trust making a family trust election or an interposed entity election is that under section 271-15 or section 271-20 of Schedule 2F to the ITAA 1936 a special tax, family trust distribution tax (FTDT), may be payable. FTDT is payable at 47% by the trustee on any conferral of present entitlement to, or distribution of, income or capital of the trust to persons who are not members of the family group of the specified individual within the meaning of section 272-90 of Schedule 2F to the ITAA 1936.

For this purpose a distribution of income or capital by a trust has the meaning given in sections 272-45 and 272-60 of Schedule 2F to the ITAA 1936.

The definition of family group includes direct family including a former spouse, a former widow or widower and a former stepchild.

If the trustee of a trust has made a family trust election or an interposed entity election and makes a payment or distribution to a beneficiary that is not subject to FTDT, you need to consider the TFN withholding for closely held trusts.

There are two main reasons to make an interposed entity election (IEE). Firstly, to make an entity a member of the family group of the individual specified in an FTE. This means that the trustee of the family trust can confer present entitlement to, or make distributions of, income or capital of the family trust on or to the entity that made the IEE without the trustee becoming liable for FTDT. Secondly, to exclude a trust from having to comply with the trustee beneficiary reporting rules in Division 6D of Part III of the *Income Tax Assessment Act 1936* (ITAA 1936).

An IEE can be made in respect of a trust that has an FTE in force. The interposed entity (company, partnership or trust) can specify an earlier income year from when the election is to commence provided that, from the beginning of the specified income year until 30th June of the income year immediately preceding that in which the election is made, both:

- the entity passes the family control test; and
- any conferrals of present entitlement to income or capital of the trust during the period, or actual distributions of such amounts, have been made on or to the individual specified in the FTE or members of that individual's family group.

Generally, an IEE is in force at all times after the 'election commencement time'.

The election commencement time is usually the beginning of the specified day in the IEE. However, if the FCT is not passed for the whole of the specified income year, the election commencement time is the earliest time from which the company, partnership or trust passes the FCT continuously for the remainder of the income year.

The death of an individual specified in an FTE of a family trust doesn't prevent any other trust, company or partnership from making an interposed entity election (IEE) to be included in that individual's family group.

A company, partnership or trust may make more than one IEE provided each family trust in respect of which the entity is making the IEE has the same individual specified in its FTE.

A family trust can make an IEE to be included in the family group of an individual who is different from the person specified in the trust's FTE, however, consequently this will effectively narrow the family group of the family trust making the IEE to those entities which are common to both specified individuals' family groups.

A super fund may make an IEE provided it passes the FCT.

As with an FTE, an IEE may start from an earlier income year to bring the entity within the family group of the specified individual. This enables the entity to access the corresponding benefits of being in the family group from the earlier income year, providing the IEE can be validly made.

As the Tax Agent, do not accept what your client asserts is the trust distribution figures without examining the appropriate documentation outlined above, notably the deed and the appropriately authorised and chronological pertinent minutes.

CHAPTER THIRTEEN

Partnerships

A partnership is a legal relationship between two or more (up to 20) people who, together, operate a business. A partnership is easy and cheap to set up and has relatively low compliance and accounting costs. A partnership needs to have an agreement or deed covering the numerous issues associated with the relationship, some of these are outlined here. A casual relationship where a deed is not consummated is highly inadvisable. The deed should be prepared by a lawyer.

The partnership requires a separate tax file number and lodges its own tax return. Partnerships are pass-through entities where the entity itself does not pay federal taxes. Instead, their income, losses, deductions and credits are passed directly to the partners, who then report their proportionate share, defined by the deed, of these items in their personal income tax returns. Regardless of whether a partnership is to be run in the names of the partners or a business name, an Australian Business Number (ABN) is required for the partnership.

As well as which partner gets what share of the income and owns which of the assets in the business, the partnership deed should also define the terms and conditions associated with the sale of the interest held by each of the partners. However, there may, in certain circumstances, be difficulty in transferring a partner's interest. The assets of the partnership are owned by the partners unless otherwise stated in the deed. The shares of the partnership firm can only be transferred once all existing partners have agreed to it. A partner's share of the capital gains or losses relating to CGT events occurring in relation to partnership assets must be disclosed on the partner's tax return. The general partners, taken together, must have at least a one percent interest in each material item of partnership income, gain, loss, deduction, or credit at all times during the existence of the partnership.

Generally, a partnership is dissolved if one of a partner dies or becomes bankrupt. The deed should outline the protocol to handle such an eventuality. It may be possible to structure it in a way where the deceased partner's executor or beneficiaries to join the partnership.

The disadvantages of a partnership include:

- potential joint liabilities;
- a loss of autonomy for one or both or all of the partners;
- emotional issues may arise just like in any marriage;
- conflict and disagreements;
- future selling complications;
- a lack of stability;
- higher taxes because company tax does not apply; and
- disputes regarding splitting profits or determining the wages of each partner.

Issues you need to look out for when preparing a partnership tax return include:

- is the partnership a small business entity (SBE) (i.e., a business that meets the $10 million aggregated turnover threshold)? If so, confirm which concessions the partnership is entitled to;
- if the partnership is an SBE, is it using the simplified depreciation rules?
- if the partnership's aggregated turnover is less than $5 million, you need to complete the 'net small business income' labels for 'small business income tax offset' purposes. The net small business income is currently in item 5, label V;
- complete each partner's 'share of net small business income' (item 51, label H);
- if the partnership is not an SBE, does it meet the $50 million aggregated turnover threshold? If so, confirm which concessions the partnership is entitled to;
- have partners' 'salaries' been excluded for tax purposes (see Taxation Ruling TR 2005/7)?
- check for any cash earnings or payments that may not have been accounted for;
- consider goods taken for own use by partners (refer Taxation Determination TD 2023/7) and the valuation of those goods;
- agree investment income e.g., dividends, interest with external source data;
- have employee contributions for FBT purposes been taken up in the accounts and appropriate GST journal entries made?

- has the partnership made or received an allocation of profits from a professional firm? If yes, consider Practical Compliance Guideline PCG 2021/4 which applies from 1 July 2022;
- put through depreciation entries and agree asset balances to depreciation schedule (including journaling asset purchases and sales);
- for asset purchases, are additions being depreciated at prime cost or diminishing value (assuming the partnership is not eligible to apply the simplified depreciation regime as the partnership is not an eligible SBE);
- perform annual entries for lease and hire purchase transactions;
- look for unusual balances of the profit and loss items (perhaps compare balances with the prior year);
- accounting fees—check against billings;
- if fees are being paid to a service entity, ensure that the service fees are within the Taxation Ruling TR 2006/2 guidelines;
- when prepayments were made during the year that cover services in the following tax year, has deductibility been determined in accordance with the prepayment rules?
- where any part of a prepayment was non-deductible in 2023 as a result of the prepayment rules, is the amount deductible in 2024?
- has entertainment expenditure been added back for tax purposes, unless it was included in the partnership's FBT return?
- have other non-deductible expenses been added back for tax purposes?

- has the partnership paid the required superannuation guarantee contributions for employees? If not, ensure that a superannuation guarantee charge statement has been lodged with the ATO;
- were employee superannuation contributions 'made' in the current income year per Taxation Ruling TR 2010/1 (to determine deductibility)?
- do wages on the income statements agree to the general ledger and activity statements lodged?
- has the payment summary information been lodged with the ATO (where required)?
- for single touch payroll purposes, has a finalisation declaration been performed for each employee?
- did the partnership fail to meet its PAYGW obligations to withhold or notify the Commissioner? If so, a deduction is denied unless the taxpayer voluntarily discloses the issue to the ATO;
- if the partnership is liable for workers compensation, have all payments been made in relevant year?
- if the partnership is not registered for payroll tax, should it be?
- has the June 2024 FBT instalment been deducted per Taxation Ruling TR 95/24?
- if the partnership is engaging contractors, have you checked whether they would be classified as employees for the purposes of PAYG withholding, superannuation guarantee, workers compensation, payroll tax, etc.?
- ensure that the financials are in line with ATO benchmarks and investigate discrepancies where necessary;
- agree bank and loan balances against statements/bank reconciliations;

- agree hire purchase balances against schedule;
- agree debtor and creditor balances;
- verify with client if all plant and equipment are still on hand (i.e., identify sales, purchases, items scrapped);
- agree trading stock figures to stock take;
- verify all other balance sheet balances;
- if the partnership derived any personal services income (PSI), is the partnership carrying on a personal services business (PSB)? If no, consider the PSI that must be attributed to an individual. If yes, consider whether the Commissioner could apply part IVA to the arrangement;
- if the partnership sold, redeemed, or disposed of an asset in any other way during the year, has the partnership advised the partners of the CGT event?
- have exemptions, reductions, or rollovers been considered?
- if there was a partnership reconstitution (e.g., admission of a new partner), has the CGT impact been considered?
- if the partnership is not registered for GST, should it be registered?
- if the partnership is registered for GST, do the GST accounts reconcile to the BAS lodged?
- does the income declared in the activity statements reconcile with the income disclosed in the tax return?
- does the partnership have transactions/loans with international related parties? If yes, consider the transfer pricing rules, and consider whether an international dealings schedule has been completed;
- does the partnership have a bank account in another country or buy/sell products offshore? If so, consider the foreign exchange rules; and
- has the partnership distribution been made in accordance with the partnership agreement?

CHAPTER FOURTEEN

Tax Planning and Business Structure Reviews

Remember every one of your business clients needs to ensure that they are paying the right amount of tax, not too much and not too little. It is critical they are structured correctly and observe practices that will achieve that goal. But the first key issue here is not to give away tax planning and organisation structure advice for free. There are liability exposures so you need to be compensated.

All tax planning advice needs to be delivered in writing. You need to keep that advice and the documents you used to support those recommendations for five years. Do not hand over the advice until you have been paid. How much you invoice should be influenced by not only how much work is involved but also by what financial benefit you believe the advice will deliver to the client rather than a one price fits all approach.

To begin the process, fully examine the recent financial performance of the entity and the tax paid as a result of that activity. Talk in detail with the client as to what they expect to obtain from your review. Go beyond just the *I want to pay less tax* into the deeper needs of the business and its owners.

Examine the current business ownership structure and obtain the reasoning behind why they structure the business in that way. At the risk of stating the obvious, obtain an ASIC listing of the company details and check with the owners whether the registered structure is what they intended it to be. Things change and in a surprising number of occasions the ASIC registered structure is not what the owners assumed it would be.

When tax planning is performed correctly it is worth the investment of your time and can be very beneficial to the client. The benefits include:

- maximising tax efficiency;
- reducing the likelihood of unexpected tax liabilities;
- allowing for tax liability funding options to be proactively considered;
- allowing for potential tax issues to be addressed before they become a problem;
- capitalising on tax incentives; and
- capitalising on opportunities to grow personal wealth.

You should start with the obvious, have a look at the business's expenses and the timing of when those expenses were taken up into the accounts. If a business is expecting to incur costs shortly after the tax year ends, then consider accruing those costs into the current year.

Consider whether all expenditure has been properly captured including expenses paid via personal credit cards or personal bank accounts.

Examine outstanding trade debtors and ask the owners to form an opinion on the recoverability of each debt and write off bad debts before the year's end. If that write off has a reasonable, documented basis it will be accepted by the ATO even if the business if required to bring it back to account the following year given circumstances change for the debtor. If it is later brought back to account, the ATO view is that they will eventually pay the tax on that income, but you must have a reasonable basis for writing the debt off in the first place.

Similarly with the trading stock that the business is carrying, if it is considered obsolete or likely to be obsolete, and that view can be substantiated, write it off in the current tax year. Again, if it is eventually sold above its written down value, even at a substantial discount, the profit margin on the sale will be taxable in the new year. It is best to advise the client to establish a written policy in regard to stock write-downs and to apply that policy consistently from year to year.

If capital gains have occurred, ensure that all available capital write-offs have been made.

Superannuation payments are only deductible if they are made prior to June 27th in the financial year. Make sure such payments are scheduled to be paid within that time frame.

Look into whether the business has taken advantage of all available tax incentive programs and ensure that going forward their systems are set up to bring the expenditures associated with these incentives to account. Some examples are:

- small business skills and training support;
- instant asset write-offs;
- export grants; and,
- research and development grants.

Where you have formed a view that the business is, or may be, entitled to R&D grants or other tax incentives (keep an eye on the professional press, new incentives come and go blown by the political winds), it is best to suggest to the owners that they bring in a specialist R&D expert, or an expert known to be proficient in obtaining these or other incentives, to prepare an application. You can't be expected to be all things to all people and that area is complex and forever changing.

Is it appropriate for the owners to consider Div 7A loans as a personal funding option or where those loans exist you need to make sure that they are supported by the appropriate documentation and that the loan recipient is abiding by the interest and principal loan repayments required by the loan agreement. Remember one of the purposes in your review is to identify and remove any potential tax liability shocks. A shareholder's loan being deemed by the ATO as non-compliant will mean that the ATO will require the full amount of the loan to be immediately taxable in the hands of the recipient. That would be quite a tax shock. Ensure that the current ATO benchmark loan interest is being used in the Div 7A loan agreements and ensure that the agreements are up to date, often further monies are drawn and the agreement isn't adjusted.

The use of a discretionary trust to hold the shares in the company is a worthwhile recommendation if they haven't already employed that device in their business structure. Distributing dividends to a discretionary trust, or multiple trusts held by each shareholder, means that the dividend distributed by the company can then be distributed in a way that best suite the shareholder's tax position. So, a typical structure should be: a company running the business, in order to take advantage of limited liability, and a discretionary trust or trusts owning the shares.

Consider also whether the business should be holding any substantial assets outside the company, and renting those assets back to the business, in order to avoid those assets being caught up in the liquidation of the company if that occurs. There is little utility in running a business as a limited liability entity if its insolvency means that substantial assets are lost in the windup.

If a trust ownership structure has been deployed, ensure that all trust resolutions regarding distributions have been made within the applicable financial year (see our chapter on trusts). The tax profile of the revenue recipients is an important consideration in determining your recommendations. Section 100A has placed renewed focus on the validity of those trust resolutions so ensure that the client is compliant.

Lastly, you need to ensure that the client is making appropriate use of personal superannuation tax concessions. At the time of writing the yearly concessional contribution was $27,500 for an individual. You should make sure, if possible, that this concession has been fully utilised. Salary sacrificed above the concessional contribution is taxed in the superfund at 15% provided that payment doesn't exceed $250,000. An additional 15% is charged on any amount above $250,000 (see Div 293).

That brings us to a consideration in the next chapter of self-managed superfunds.

CHAPTER FIFTEEN

Self-Managed Super Funds, SMSF

You will encounter clients who want to know whether a self-managed superfund, SMSF, is the right choice for them instead of them paying into a managed fund. The answer isn't straightforward and lately the regulations relating to SMSF have been changing rapidly so you need to be well informed regarding the current compliance regulations.

Some of your clients will like the idea of controlling their own super funds but there are pitfalls. They can own property in the fund, except their own home, so it has to be property owned for commercial purposes, and the ownership of the property has to be structured properly—usually through a bare trust. If, after discussion and due consideration, your client wants to set up a SMSF, then give the setup task to a licensed financial planner who will also brief your client on their obligations as trustee of the fund and create for them an appropriate investment plan. A formal investment plan is legally required where the value of the real estate held by the fund exceeds 5% of the money under management. The planner will insist on billing the client directly for that service. All funds held by the client in their name in an industry fund can be transferred by the planner into their own new SMSF without penalty.

You, the Tax Agent, can do the bookkeeping for the fund and the end of year reporting including the tax return for which you will be paid fees out of the fund. Those end-of-year compliance reports need to be audited by a licensed auditor, typically before you complete the tax return. Waiting to do the tax return until after the audit is advisable because it means that you will only have to do it once.

The generation of the compliance and end-of-year reporting based on your bookkeeping is a specialised task but you are legally permitted to do it provided you know how. The audit of those end-of-year reports requires a licensed auditor. There is specialised software for the administration and bookkeeping task, BGL being the most common in Australia, but frankly you may be better off handing over the end-of-year compliance reporting, except the tax return, to one of the myriads of specialist firms who provide that service. They are up to date with the requirements, have the specialised software—which isn't cheap—and because of the number of firms competing in that space the price you can obtain for that service makes it cost effective for you to use it. I do mean *you* using the service, you should farm out that work and the audit and have those firms bill you. You then bill the client for the bookkeeping, the provision of the end of year reports, the audit and the tax return. Most firms offering the end-of-year compliance work do not do the tax return because they often don't have a licensed Tax Agent on staff, but they almost always will package up the audit for you in their price. So, in the end you get the audited end-of-year compliance pack and a listing from their software, usually BGL, for you to use to confidently base you tax return.

Your client will expect you to understand why they should or should not create a SMSF and they will rely on your advice as to whether they should set one up.

The disadvantages of having a SMSF are: the responsibility of compliance, the breaching of which brings severe financial and sometimes criminal penalties, the limited ability to diversify sufficiently to minimise market risk (because of the smaller amount of money under management) and the lack of a compensation scheme (life or disability insurance) but their financial planner can advise them on perhaps including insurance.

The cost of the fund is also a consideration, including the initial setup costs and the fees you intend to charge for the bookkeeping, the end-of-year compliance reporting, the audit, and the tax return. But keep in mind the client doesn't avoid those costs if they are using a managed fund, they do pay administration surcharges in an industry fund. If the SMSF holds over $250,000 the administrative cost of running it is usually equivalent or less than an industry fund.

There is no minimum balance required to be held in a SMSF other than the cost effectiveness just mentioned. The general individual concessional contributions cap is the same as paying into an industry fund, $27,500 at the time of writing.

There are some benefits in that an SMSF allows more choice of investment strategies including property, art, coins and gold. The financial advisor can discuss their options and advise them on those things in which they are not permitted to invest. Included in those not permitted investments is buying their own home. The type of property, if held, must be exclusively and wholly used for business - think commercial properties, office buildings, or factories. So, an SMSF can offer several advantages, including investment control, tax management, estate planning and potentially lower fees for large account balances. However, the downsides involve the time and effort to manage the fund, compliance risks, limited diversification and restricted access to government protections.

Just like the industry funds, the tax rate for income earned by the SMSF is currently 15%. When the income is used to provide a pension stream, there is no tax at all. However, these concessions are available only to funds that comply with the ATO's requirements for SMSFs.

CHAPTER SIXTEEN

Payroll

Payroll is becoming an increasingly complex process as the ATO persistently adds new requirements for businesses as they hand back more and more tax collection and compliance tasks to the business owner. This means that if you are intending to offer payroll as part of your tax services, you or one of your staff is going to have to remain up to date with these changes and be knowledgeable about, and stay compliant with, the current payroll legislation. You need to be a registered BAS Agent or Tax Agent to offer payroll services to the general public.

I'm going to give you an overview of the process and the requirements of providing a payroll service but, as is the case with this textbook, the specific tax and compliance issues should only be considered as a general guide because of the constant changes in the legislation.

In Australia, three basic payroll systems are used: manual payroll, outsourced payroll and in-house payroll software.

- Manual payroll: this is usually processed using spreadsheets, or paper-based systems design specifically for making the manual task easier for the user. It involves manual calculations and physical timesheets. This method is not only time-consuming but also prone to errors and inefficiencies. Manual payroll, however, has become redundant because of the ATO's Single Touch Payroll (STP) requirements. You or your client will now need some kind of payroll software.

- Outsourced payroll: this means that an external specialist resource is hired by the small business owner to manage everything starting from client records to wages reports and the payroll taxes.
- Payroll software: usually, a modern software system offers everything, starting from basic payroll assistance to other services like time tracking.

Before choosing the ideal system for payroll, consider different factors like business growth, employee benefits, business efficiency, cost and the complexity of your state's payroll taxes.

All Australian employers must be familiar with the relevant industry awards and the National Employment Standards (NES). Awards don't apply when there is a registered enterprise in place but the National Employment Standards still apply. No employment contract can provide less than the relevant award.

Before finalising the payroll policies and procedures, the foremost step is to review the local labour laws, state overtime laws and federal labour laws. One of the most common FLSA violations is unpaid overtime, which is most likely to happen when you don't know the rules.

A few things to add to your payroll policy:

- pay dates may also include the length of each pay period and the day when you pay the employees;
- how you are going to pay employees; and
- information about payroll deductions and withholdings and how this can benefit your offer will impact employees' pays.

An employer must have, and the employee needs to be aware of the following:

- full name and address;
- employee tax file number;
- next of kin contact details;
- start date;
- a signed payroll tax declaration;
- written agreement on the following:
  - form of employment—full-time, part-time or casual;
  - annual or hourly salary with deductions as per contract;
  - allowances, bonuses or benefits that the employee receives as per contract;
  - leave entitlements as detailed on contract subject to any registered agreement, industry award or NEWs (in that order);
- employee super fund details namely superfund name and membership number, ABN and USI; and,
- payment details (employee bank account).

If your payroll has benefits like health insurance or retirement savings, you will need documents to show that the employee also has approved those additional deductions.

Payroll tax is a state tax paid on wages exceeding certain thresholds, different states have different threshold, e.g., In Victoria 2023/2024 FY it is $700,000 yearly or $58,333 monthly.

You should set up a direct deposit to pay the employees, it's the most common mode of payment because it's convenient for both employees and employers. An employer can set up a direct deposit through the business's bank directly or via the payroll service provider. If the employees opt for the direct deposit, they'll have to provide information like the bank's name, account number, account type (checking or savings) and your bank's routing number.

Personal super deductions for a sole trader and individuals require an intent to claim form request to superfunds before tax returns are lodged. Superfunds will usually send two confirmations that the application has been received and the tax withheld. The tax return should not be lodged until the second confirmation has been received, otherwise the client may lose the right to claim the contribution as a tax deduction. Be aware of the differences in tax rates between resident and non-resident for tax purposes, part-year tax free thresholds and minor or exempted income.

It is advisable for the employer to set up a time tracking system. An employer must maintain accurate records of work hours for all non-exempted employees. In most cases, the non-exempt employees are paid hourly. To keep these records, you can track the hours manually and ask the employees to write down when they start working. Otherwise, you can use time tracking software for maintaining employee timesheet records. Either way, you can train your employees to track their time. Before starting the first payroll, collect the employee timecards. In the case of paper timecards, the process of calculation and checking for errors can be lengthy. However, if you opt for payroll software, the process becomes seamless and faster.

Getting approval to process a payroll once it has been completed for the period is one of the crucial steps when running payroll for hourly employees. During this process, you must check the authenticity of the hours invested by the employee. Once all the employee timecards are checked, you can run the payroll and issue payments to the employees. It is best that the person processing the payroll is not the one authorising the release of payments.

Once you have initiated the wage payments, it is time to update the payroll records. The records must show that the federal income is withheld by you and Medicare taxes from employee wages. You will also be required to show the tax contributions made. There are variations in contribution arrangements:

- the standard working week in Australia is 38 hours. However, an employer can make reasonable requests to employees to work beyond their allotted hours. But in this case, the employer must pay overtime of 150% of the hourly rate for the first three hours. And 200% must be paid for work undertaken on Sundays, unless the award states otherwise;

- employers must also take care of the worker's compensation insurance in case of accidents incurred at the workplace. It is not uncommon for clients to have their Tax Agent prepare the annual Workcover declaration;

- an employer must pay severance pay to employees who have to stay for at least a year. The rates may differ between four and 16 weeks of salary, depending on the length of employment and the state in which they work. The business owner needs to ensure that they are complying with the required severance arrangements;

- an employer has to contribute 12% (the 2025/26 rate), 11.5% at time of writing, for superannuation which is usually remitted quarterly to the relevant institutions, monthly once the payroll rises above a certain amount, or it can be voluntarily be paid monthly by the employer. Payday Super is coming on the 1st July, 2026. If the business owner wants the superannuation to be a deductible expense in any given tax year, the superannuation payments must be in sufficient time for it to be received into the employee's super account unless the employer is using the ATO super clearing house in which the payment needs to be made by the 28th June but the clearing house if closing on the 1st July, 2026; and

- an employee is entitled to four weeks of paid leave every year. In addition to this, there is long service leave and paid parental leave, sick leave and domestic violence leave, pro rata for permanent employees only.

According to the payroll policies and procedures in Australia, the employees are paid on a weekly, bi-monthly, or monthly basis. There are no specific requirements regarding the time when an employee needs to be paid. However, some of the standard payroll cycles followed in Australia are:

- monthly—from the 28th to the 30th of the month;
- bi-weekly—every second week on any agreed day (usually it is Wednesday or Thursday); and
- bi-monthly—Every 15th and 30th.

In Australia, an employee is entitled to the following benefits:

- holiday allowance: these are paid days off given on public holidays. In exceptional cases, the employees can be asked to work;
- annual leave: 4 weeks of paid leave every year is given to an employee. In addition to this, an extra week is given to shift workers;
- community service eave: under this, an employee can get up to 10 days of paid leave for the jury service. (After ten days, it is unpaid) In addition, unpaid leave is also provided for voluntary emergency work; and
- medical leave: an employee is entitled to 10 days of paid personal (sick) or caregiver's leave, two days of unpaid caregiver's leave and two days of compassionate leave.

Termination payments vary from state to state and you need to comply with what is outlined as a pre-modernised applicable award. The development of a uniform national long service leave standard is still pending.

Single Touch Payroll (STP) is an Australian Government initiative to streamline employers' reporting to government agencies. With STP you report employees' payroll information to the ATO each time you pay them through STP-enabled software. Payroll information includes:

- salaries and wages;
- pay as you go (PAYG) withholding; and
- superannuation liability information.

STP started on 1st July 2018 for employers with 20 or more employees and 1st July 2019 for employers with 19 or fewer employees and is now a mandatory obligation. From 1st January

2022, the data collected through STP was expanded (known as STP Phase 2) to collect additional payroll information. All employers should now be STP reporting and transitioned to STP Phase 2 reporting unless covered by an exemption.

If the client is new to employing, you will need to go through STP Phase 2 enabled software as soon as you start paying your employees to avoid any penalties.

STP works by sending tax and super information from your STP-enabled payroll or accounting software directly to the ATO when you run the payroll. You will:

- run your payroll;
- pay your employees as normal; and
- give them a payslip.

The pay cycle doesn't need to change. The client can continue to pay your employees weekly, fortnightly or monthly. The STP-enabled payroll software will send us a report that includes the information we need from you, such as:

- salaries and wages;
- PAYG withholding; and
- super liability information.

There are several ways you can report STP data. STP Phase 2 doesn't change the payments you need to report through STP but it does change how those amounts need to be reported. Full lists of the payments that must be reported in STP Phase 1 and STP Phase 2 are available in the STP employer reporting guidelines.

Super funds also report to the ATO. They let them know when the client makes the super payment to your employees' chosen or default fund. This is an important step toward making sure employees are paid their correct entitlements. The ATO systems will match the STP information to the employer and employee records.

At the end of the financial year, the client needs to finalise its STP data. This means the client is making a declaration that they have completed their reporting for the financial year. Once it finalises the data the employee's income statement in ATO online services will be marked as *Tax Ready*. They, or their registered agent, will be able use the income statement to lodge their tax return.

With STP the client doesn't need to provide employee payment summaries or provide us with a payment summary annual report for amounts you report through STP.

STP data reported by employers is shared. The ATO exchanges data with Services Australia and other government agencies to support the administration of the welfare system and other services.

If employees have a MyGov account linked to ATO online services, they will be able to see their year-to-date tax and super information in their income statement. Their data is updated every time you report. For most employers, this will be each pay day.

There is certain information that your client needs to give their employees, which include superannuation fund standard choice form and the Fair Work Information Statement. Your client needs to be aware of and compliant with each state's industrial legislation, awards, the national minimum employment standards and Workcover for their employees. Most states have a website that provides helpful information on these obligations.

CHAPTER SEVENTEEN

Tax Agent Services Regulations (TASR)
ETHICS

TASR are the governing regulations regarding your conduct as a Tax Agent or BAS Agent. It is regularly updated, so you need to keep an eye out for TPB pronouncements on ethics. In very broad terms the regulation requires:

1. Honesty and integrity:

    - you must act honestly and with integrity;
    - you must comply with the taxation laws in the conduct of your own personal affairs; and
    - if you receive money or other property from or on behalf of a client, and hold the money or other property on trust, you must account to your client for the money or other property.

2. Independence:

    - you must act lawfully in the best interests of your client; and
    - you must have in place adequate arrangements for the management of conflicts of interest that may arise in

relation to the activities that you undertake in the capacity of a registered Tax Agent.

3. Confidentiality:

    - unless you have a legal duty to do so, you must not disclose any information relating to a client's affairs to a third party without your client's permission.

4. Competence:

    - you must ensure that a Tax Agent service that you provide, or that is provided on your behalf, is provided competently;
    - you must maintain knowledge and skills relevant to the Tax Agent services that you provide;
    - you must take reasonable care in ascertaining a client's state of affairs, to the extent that ascertaining the state of those affairs is relevant to a statement you are making or a thing you are doing on behalf of a client; and
    - you must take reasonable care to ensure that taxation laws are applied correctly to the circumstances in relation to which you are providing advice to a client.

5. Other responsibilities:

    - you must not knowingly obstruct the proper administration of the taxation laws;
    - you must advise your client of the client's rights and obligations under the taxation laws that are materially related to the Tax Agent services you provide;
    - you must maintain the professional indemnity insurance that the board requires you to maintain;

- you must respond to requests and directions from the board in a timely, responsible and reasonable manner;
- you must not employ, or use the services of, an entity to provide Tax Agent services on your behalf if:
  - you know, or ought reasonably to know, that the entity is a disqualified entity; and
  - the board has not given you approval under Section 45-5 to employ or use the services of the disqualified entity to provide Tax Agent services on your behalf;
- you must not provide Tax Agent services in connection with an arrangement with an entity that you know, or ought reasonably to know, is a disqualified entity; and
- you must comply with any obligations determined under Section 30-12.

The national authority for enforcing these regulations is the Tax Practitioners Board (TPB), to whom you will be applying for your Tax Agent or BAS Agent license. They conduct investigations of any breach of the regulations and impose administrative sanctions for non-compliance including the cancellation of your license.

You will be required to make an annual declaration to the TPB that you have meet all your obligations including your professional development study in order to have your license renewed.

At time of writing the TPB require 120 hours of accredited study (CPE) over a three-year period.

Keeping up with the taxation regulations and with industry standards is a critical part of your responsibilities as a Tax Agent or BAS Agent. You can't provide informed advice or quality services to your clients unless you are up to date with your study. In the writer's opinion, the 120 hours is the rock-bottom minimum study that you should undertake. In order to adjunct this study, make a point of joining local tax-profession discussion groups.

All Tax Agents and BAS Agents are required by the TPB to carry an appropriate amount (relevant to turnover) of Professional Indemnity Insurance (PI). An accredited insurance provider can advise you on the size of the cover that you are required to maintain. One of the areas where being a member of a professional association is the bulk purchase of insurance allowing their members to enjoy worthwhile discounts when acquiring PI insurance.

At the time of writing, the relevant professional associations accredited with the TPB are:

- CPA Australia;
- Institute of Public Accountants (IPA);
- Chartered Accountants Australia and NZ (CA);
- National Tax Agents Association (NTAA);
- The Tax Institute (TTI); and
- Financial Planners Association of Australia.

There are fourteen in all but these are the ones most relevant to being a Tax Agent. You will not be required to join a professional association (RPA) in order to apply for a license but your membership of one of them is well-regarded by the TPB and they are useful in providing CPE courses, keeping you abreast of legislative changes, assisting with certain specialised technical questions and, as mentioned above, assisting you with your insurance requirements.

A Tax Agent is required to lodge 85% or more of their clients' current year tax returns by the due date. If you don't, you'll get a call from the TPB and they will agree with you any appropriate actions.

If you are registered as a tax practitioner, your registration may be terminated if:

- any of the following events occur:
  - you are convicted of a serious taxation offence;
  - you are convicted of an offence involving fraud or dishonesty;
  - you are penalised for being a promoter of a tax exploitation scheme;
  - you are penalised for implementing a scheme that has been promoted on the basis of conformity with a product ruling in a way that is materially different from that described in the product ruling;
  - you become an undischarged bankrupt; or
  - you are sentenced to a term of imprisonment.
- you cease to meet one of the tax practitioner registration requirements;
- you breach a condition of your registration (if they were imposed); or
- you breach the Code of Professional Conduct.

The TPB must also terminate your registration if:

- you surrender your registration by written notice unless they consider that, due to a current investigation or the outcome of an investigation, it would be inappropriate to terminate your registration; or
- you die.

A failure to comply with a written notice is a breach of the code.

CHAPTER EIGHTEEN

Other Statutory Reporting Requirements

To properly fulfill your function as a public practitioner there are other governmental obligations that your clients need to fulfill on a regular basis other than reporting to the ATO and to ASIC. You clients will expect you to know what these are and how to meet those obligations.

Do not give these tasks away to your clients and write them off as simple add-ons to the end of year tax task. These are all important jobs that need to be done for your clients with trusts or companies and in some cases sole trader businesses. These tasks are all chargeable so have each service on your price list and ensure that your clients keep them up to date.

1. Keep track of all company and trust minutes, particularly trust minutes related to the distribution of income.

2. Remind your clients of all upcoming lodgement deadlines including the payment of superannuation.

3. NSW has an annual lodgement system were the current balances of long service leave (LSL) needs to be reported to the government.

4. For individuals, you need to lodge a NAT71121 Notice of Intent to claim superannuation deductions.

5. An entity that hires subcontractors needs to complete a Reportable Subcontractor Payments (TPAR) statement. If your client operates a business that is "primarily in the building and construction industry, has an ABN and makes payments to contractor's", you're required to lodge a Taxable Payments Annual Report (TPAR) every year. Contractors can include subcontractors, consultants and independent contractors. They can operate as sole traders (individuals), companies, partnerships or trusts but be aware that if the contractor is acting as a sole trader the ATO may deem them to be employees bring obligation for your client to withhold PAYG, pay superannuation and other entitlements. A TPAR needs to be lodged to the Australian Taxation Office (ATO) by 28th August every year. The report is a summary of payments made to contractors for building and construction services provided. Payments made to suppliers also needs to be reported in cases where you have paid for more than just a product, for instance, if you hire an excavator with an operator, you need to report the payment made to the hire company.

6. GST Annual Return—if you are voluntarily registered for GST and have not made an election to pay GST by instalments check your options.

7. There are a number of tasks associated with the lodgement of the BAS:

   - simpler BAS reporting method;
   - reporting other tax obligations annually;

- how to elect to report GST annually;
- when you can make your election;
- when your election takes effect;
- check your eligibility each year;
- when your election ceases to have effect;
- when to lodge your annual GST return; and
- making early payments.

8. Self-review non-charitable not-for-profits (NFPs) with an active ABN need to lodge an annual NFP self-review return to confirm their eligibility to self-assess as income tax exempt. You may not need to lodge if your NFP is:

- a certain type of government entity;
- an Australian Charities and Not-for-profit Commission (ACNC) type of entity, as it cannot self-assess income tax exemption; or
- an NFP sub-entity (for GST purposes).

9. QBCC—Queensland Building Construction Commission. If you work in the building industry in Queensland, chances are you need a licence. They have clear definitions of when you do need a licence and the criteria to be eligible to hold a licence and this applies to all kinds of business entities. The QBCC has a number of public registers, some required by law and others relating to the functions of QBCC for further information go to the website Home Queensland Building and Construction Commission.

10. Payroll tax—payroll tax is a state or territory tax. It is calculated on the total wages, the thresholds for which vary from state to state. In NSW for example the current threshold is $1,200,000 and the rate is 5.45%. The state or territory that

your employees are located in collects the tax. Thresholds and tax rates vary between states and territories. You need to register for payroll tax if your total Australian wages are more than the threshold. Check the threshold for each state or territory where you have employees. You can find the threshold and payroll tax rate on the state or territory revenue office website.

Your clients will expect you to know how to make these lodgements, when they are applicable and when they are due. If one is missed it will undoubtably be your fault, particularly if your client gets fined.

Keep a close eye on the administrative burdens such as these placed on you client by the various authorities, there are more coming.

CHAPTER NINETEEN

Final Reminders of Risks and Issues

First and foremost, do not be cheap. Cheap is the road to failure for public practitioners for so many reasons. Low margins mean a low per hour pay to you and consequently, it means you can't afford the necessary time to keep yourself up to date with the task law or be diligent in your tax return preparation and reviews. Being cheap also brings other exposures. Consider what kind of clients wants a cheap service: transients who will shop you every year so you'll never build a client base, and clients who want a low, or worse still, a manipulated tax payable, they may even go as far as providing you with incomplete or inaccurate information to obtain a better tax payable result. If they do, you will spend an inordinate amount of time explaining yourself to the ATO. Equally important, cheap clients think they own you and will exploit your time. High paying clients understand that the service transaction is a fee for service, so they will pay the right price for the right level of service. Cheap clients don't understand that reality. Seeking out cheap clients means that you are robbing yourself of the margin you need to build your business and your lifestyle.

Cheap clients are not only scamming you they are usually also trying to scam the tax office. They will eventually get caught and the ATO will be asking you why you didn't catch on. Sure, you can hide behind the fact that you are not an auditor, and the client signed and therefor took responsibility for the tax return but the ATO expects you to be 'diligent'. After such an incident they will be watching you and it doesn't take much for you to lose your livelihood. Clients who pressure you to provide a manipulated tax result are trouble and they will get you in trouble. Send them on their way.

One of the key issues related to pricing is to ensure that you don't give services away. Unlike many businesses you don't have stock sitting on shelves burning a hole in your pocket. But you need to consider your time and the time of your staff in the same light. Does a general store owner hand out free stock to their customers? The trap to avoid here is looking like a miserly cash grabber to your clients if you charge them for every ten minutes with you on the phone. The way to avoid that is to have your service packages listed and priced, including your and your staff's hourly rates, and ensure your clients sign off on your engagement letter and that price list. Ensure that they know where the line is between a quick, perhaps free, enquiry and a time-consuming review that requires you to provide formal written advice. If that casual phone conversation develops into a regular attempt by your client to get free advice, professionally advise them of the fact that they need to pay for your time, like they expect their clients to do. In all of that keep in mind that the new ethics guidelines from the ATO require you to put all tax advice in writing and keep that correspondence with supporting information for five years. All that takes time—your time.

I had a very wealthy client once who wasn't, as far as I could tell, all that smart. I couldn't figure out how he became so successful, he was a very wealthy self-made man. I eventually figured it out, and it became a key business lesson for me in my own business. This guy's superpower was his ability to recognise very early that something wasn't working, and he was very quick to get rid of it, and by that I mean disinvest, or change a procedure or marketing initiative or a staff member that wasn't paying off. Most business people will hold onto something that they have invested time or money in or committed to until they go down with the ship. That is not a good business practice and your lack of willingness to recognise the problem early and act quickly to fix it is a very real exposure to your business. This principle particularly applies to the staff you hire. Whilst you must always follow the employment regulations, you need to make sure that you are investing your time, money and trust in the right people.

Keep in touch with your local business owners and network with them and other professionals to stay in touch with their needs and to continually reevaluate your service offering. Regularly post to your social media accounts, or have one of your staff do it, to let your local businesses and your clients know that you are running a vibrant practice and to keep both your existing clients and prospective clients up to date with your service offerings. The more they see you, the more work you'll get.

Keep a close eye on your cash flows and remember to base your expenditures on real income, not prospective income.

Constantly bring your business costs back to market. Avoid the temptation of staying with a supplier because you can't be bothered to test the market out because of some misplaced delusion of loyalty. Look after your business, let your suppliers look after their own service levels and pricing.

Learn to say no. As a general rule say no when it involves further expenditure on something you are not already doing. Evaluate very carefully any additional expenditures and that includes adding more staff. Don't get distracted by inconsequential rubbish or add-ons that don't improve your business profitability. One of the businesspeople who I came to admire had the habit when acquiring a new business, or reevaluating one he already owned, of cancelling all subscriptions, artificial plant hire, rubber mat services and any other ongoing subscription-based expenditure as well as immediately tendering all service contracts. He told me that he was always available to discuss those cancellation with any staff member who insisted that the service or subscription was required. But he said that, unsurprisingly, nobody ever turned up at his door to argue the point.

Stay balanced and purposeful. Remind yourself of why you are doing what you are doing. Build an asset rather than get buried under it.

Be very careful when you are employing people. Make sure they are a good fit not only for the task requirements but also with the practice culture. They need to get along with your existing staff. I have always maintained that it must be a requirement that they be nice people, however you define that term, partly because nice people are usually honest but mainly nice people maintain a harmonious environment in the office. The last thing you need is to be distracted by conflict in the office.

Always put new staff on a trial period of at least three months, keeping them on casual status until the trial period is over before you put them on permanently either part-time or full-time. Make sure your employment contracts are solid and that you have passed these by your lawyer. Clearly define staff roles and job functions and monitor their performance against those objectives. Train them and mentor them, don't just throw them in the deep end.

Do not offer credit to your clients, you are not their banker you are their Tax Agent. Avoid, where at all possible, any kind of debt. Let the practice grow organically and insist that it feeds itself the capital that it needs.

Be quick to identify clients who:

- are wasting your time;
- who are exhibiting a tendency to cut corners with their accounting;
- who want you to cut corners with their tax liabilities; or,
- who are slow payers.

They are a distraction and a burden. Don't be afraid to ask them to leave, politely, once you have identified them.

Ensure that you stay up to date with tax law changes and with service trends in the industry including computerisation and AI. It is not just a requirement of the ATO that you stay up to date, you have an obligation to your clients to ensure that they are paying the right amount of tax and nothing more, that they are paying you a fair price and getting value for service, and that they are meeting all their reporting obligations to the government.

Good luck building your business and know that you have joined a prestigious and fulfilling career path.

The considerable resources of Tax Agent Pathway (www.taxagentpathway.com.au) are available to you to assist you with the supervision you may need to get your relevant work experience in order to obtain your own Tax Agent or BAS Agent license and to help you establish and create a successful practice.